Software Quality

*A Framework
for Success in
Software Development
and Support*

ACM PRESS BOOKS

Editor-in-Chief   **Peter Wegner**   Brown University
International Editor **Dines Bjørner**   Technical University
(Europe)   of Denmark

SELECTED TITLES

Object-Oriented Reuse, Concurrency and Distribution
  Colin Atkinson

Advances in Database Programming Languages   *Francois Bançilhon
  and Peter Buneman (Eds)*

Algebraic Specification   *J.A. Bergstra, J. Heering and P. Klint (Eds)*

Software Reusability (Volume 1: Concepts and Models)
  Ted Biggerstaff and Alan Perlis (Eds)

Software Reusability (Volume 2: Applications and Experience)
  Ted Biggerstaff and Alan Perlis (Eds)

Object-Oriented Software Engineering: A Use Case Driven Approach
  Ivar Jacobson, Magnus Christerson, Patrik Jonnson and Gunnar Övergaard

Object-Oriented Concepts, Databases and Applications
  Won Kim and Frederick H. Lochovsky (Eds)

Distributed Systems (2nd edn)   *Sape Mullender (Ed)*

Computing: A Human Activity   *Peter Naur*

The Oberon System: User Guide and Programmer's Manual   *Martin Reiser*

Programming in Oberon: Steps Beyond Pascal and Modula   *Martin Reiser and
  Niklaus Wirth*

The Programmer's Apprentice   *Charles Rich and Richard C. Waters*

User Interface Design   *Harold Thimbleby*

Project Oberon: The Design of an Operating System and Compiler   *Niklaus
  Wirth and Jürg Gutknecht*

Software Quality

A Framework
for Success in
Software Development
and Support

JOC SANDERS

EUGENE CURRAN

Centre for Software Engineering, Dublin

Addison-Wesley Publishing Company

Wokingham, England • Reading, Massachusetts • Menlo Park, California
New York • Don Mills, Ontario • Amsterdam • Bonn • Sydney • Singapore
Tokyo • Madrid • San Juan • Milan • Paris • Mexico City • Seoul • Taipei

Cover designed by Arthur op den Brouw, Reading
and printed by The Riverside Printing Co. (Reading) Ltd.
Printed and bound in Great Britain by T.J. Press (Padstow) Ltd, Cornwall.

First printed 1994. Reprinted 1995.

ISBN 0–201–63198–9

British Library Cataloguing-in-Publication Data
A catalogue record for this book is available from the British Library.

Library of Congress Cataloging-in-Publication Data is available

Foreword

Led by theorists such as Shewart, Deming and Juran, practitioners at Toyota, Honda, Xerox, Ford and many other firms around the world have changed our expectations for quality – both as consumers and producers. As consumers we have come to regard defects as unacceptable. We expect products to work 'out of the box' and to give long and reliable service. We also expect them to anticipate and meet our real needs, to be easy to use, and to be flexible for change and modification (as in modular stereo, camera and computer systems). Products that do not measure up to these standards are considered 'second class' or 'cut-rate' and can only demand cut-rate prices. They will not be considered competitive in a global marketplace.

As producers, our relation to quality has also changed. Our old theory was that defects are inevitable, and that a certain number should be allowed to get to the customer in order to maximize profitability! We now realise that there is no inherent limit to the level of quality that can be achieved. However, we have also learned that the secret to continuously increasing quality is not more stringent testing but a continuously improving quality process. In other words, the new rule is 'build quality in' instead of 'test defects out'. But quality is a challenge that requires a commitment from the entire firm, and a detailed plan of action. Fortunately, much has been learned over the last 30 years about how to build a 'quality system' across a wide variety of businesses.

Not too surprisingly, the lessons learned initially in the manufacturing sector, and which are now being applied to many service and white collar activities, are only beginning to be applied to software development. We have a long history of resisting the analysis and redesign of our own processes, even as we analyze and automate the processes of our brethren in other professions. We still accept defects as part and parcel of the product. Rather than issuing a warranty that our products are defect-free, we include a disclaimer disavowing ourselves from responsibility. Surely something is wrong here.

Fortunately, the European Community is actively encouraging the institutionalization of software quality by promoting the ISO 9000 family of standards, which describes what is required of a satisfactory quality system. ISO 9000 is widely recognized in Europe and is rapidly gaining acceptance in the US and many other parts of the world. It promises to become the global standard by which the government, industrial and private consumers can judge the fitness of suppliers. It can also serve as the blueprint by which suppliers can achieve the quality level they desire. Happily, ISO 9000 contains components specifically targeted for software development, and these are the topic of *Software Quality: A Framework for Success in Software Development and Support*.

In this clear, concise and highly-informative text, Joc Sanders and Eugene Curran provide a 'nuts-and-bolts' guide for managers who might ask the question, 'Why bother with ISO 9000 anyway?' Starting with a bottom-line business rationale, *Framework for Success* explains why quality will be a key competitive factor in the coming years – not just in Europe, but around the world.

They map out the definition of quality in operational terms, explain the many business benefits it can produce, and lay the responsibility for achieving it squarely at the feet of top management. Fortunately for wary managers, Sanders and Curran don't stop there. *Framework for Success* also explains how to implement a Quality System throughout the company, from assessing the organization, right through establishing procedures, support activities, certification and training. Besides explaining how each of these topics affect software quality, the book provides a useful summary of ISO 9000 itself, and relates ISO 9000 to essential quality characteristics and good engineering principles.

It's time for the software industry to come out of the 'middle ages' and establish industrial-strength processes every bit as robust, reliable and economical as those now in use in manufacturing and service sectors. *Software Quality: A Framework for Success in Software Development and Support* is an excellent place to start understanding how you can employ ISO 9000 to reach your quality goals, and to achieve certification under an international standard at the same time.

Gene Forte
Executive Editor
CASE OUTLOOK

Preface

Why this book is the way it is

This book does not pretend to be a comprehensive, academic text, telling you all that you could ever want to know about software quality, and more. If it did, it would be much bigger, and you would probably find it difficult to sift the important grain from the detailed chaff! Instead, we have written a *guidebook* with the clear objective of meeting the *practical* needs of busy software engineers and their managers, working in real-world businesses. We believe these needs are for a concise, readable book, with separate parts addressed to two audiences:

Part 1 is a Manager's Guide to Implementing a Quality System. It gives high-level guidance on why and how to implement a Quality System in a software organization. It also explains how to seek certification for it, and gives up-to-date information about the ISO 9000 international standards for quality systems and alternatives to them. It is for managers who are planning or initiating a software quality programme, but it will also be of interest to practising software engineers wanting an introduction to software quality management.

Part 2 is a Software Engineer's Guide to Best Practice. It presents a guide to current best practice, drawn from a variety of current international standards on software engineering, and also addresses software support services. It can be used as a checklist during a software quality programme, both to assess actual practice and to define the objectives of proposed new practices.

We have considered the needs of large, medium and small organizations, without compromising the requirements of the international quality standards applicable to software, namely ISO 9001, ISO 9000-3, and ISO 9004-2. And we believe the guidance we have given is relevant to all types of software organizations, from commercial software houses, to management information systems departments in user companies, to the developers of real-time and embedded systems.

We hope that many companies will be able to use our book as a basis from which to develop their own quality system by themselves. Others may need expert advice and assistance as well. Our book may not contain all the answers you need, but it will set you off in the right direction.

The underlying philosophy

We have found it useful when starting to read a book, or when deciding whether to buy it, to have some idea of the authors' underlying approach and philosophy. It helps the reader to evaluate what is likely to be relevant to him or her. So we feel it is proper for us to declare some of the propositions and beliefs which we have arrived at over the years, as working software managers and engineers ourselves. We summarize them as follows:

- Quality is the key to success in the software business, as it is in every other.
- The cheapest way to improve software productivity is to improve software quality.
- The quality of software support is as important as the quality of the software product: the support environment must be engineered as carefully as the software itself.
- To achieve software quality, people and culture are as important as technology – if not more so.
- The only way to improve software quality reliably is to improve the software process (which includes personnel, facilities, equipment, technology and methodology).
- Process improvement is usually unsuccessful unless top management demonstrate genuine commitment and leadership.
- Quality and process improvement are an unrelenting endeavour: it is always possible to do it a little better, a little faster, a little cheaper.
- An ISO 9000-compliant quality system is a good early target for many software organizations, but not for all.
- A software organization's quality system must be tailored to its specific needs and circumstances or it will not be both effective and efficient.
- An effective software quality system uses good software engineering practices, based on the following principles:

Quality principles
 – Try to prevent defects from being introduced in the first place
 – Ensure defects that get in are detected and corrected as early as

possible
- Establish and eliminate the causes as well as the symptoms of defects
- Independently audit work for compliance with standards and procedures

Management principles
- Define roles and responsibilities
- Plan the work
- Track progress against the plans and take corrective action where necessary
- Progressively refine the plans

Engineering principles
- Analyze the problem before developing the solution
- Break complex problems into several less complex ones
- Ensure the subproblems knit together by controlling their relationships.

Acknowledgements

The first draft of this book was written as part of an Irish national initiative, co-ordinated by the National Software Directorate, with support from the European Community Structural Funds. Without their support, and the support of the Centre for Software Engineering for which we both work, this book would not have been possible.

Our thanks are due to the very many individuals, who have helped us meet our objective by reviewing early drafts and providing a wealth of valuable comments. They are too numerous to mention by name, but include many colleagues in the Irish software industry, and the staff of Addison-Wesley, our publishers. Such merits as this book displays are in large part due to them, while its defects are of course our own!

Lastly, we are very conscious of the enormous debt that we each owe to those who have gone before us. Some of these are acknowledged in the bibliography in Appendix B, but we recall here also all those friends, teachers and colleagues from whom we have learned everything that we know.

Joc Sanders
Eugene Curran
Centre for Software Engineering
Dublin, Ireland

Contents

Part 1

Manager's Guide to Implementing a Quality System

Part 1 of this book gives guidance for managers of software organizations on why and how to implement a quality system, and how to seek certification for it.

Chapter 1 defines what we mean by software quality, and what a quality system is. Chapter 2 deals with the human and cultural issues which are so vital for success. Chapter 3 explains how to implement a quality system, using a straight-forward five-step model. Chapter 4 discusses how to demonstrate the effectiveness of the quality system either by obtaining ISO 9000 certification, or using other sources.

Part 1

Manager's Guide to Implementing a Quality System

1
Defining Software Quality

1.1   Why Bother With Quality?

Why bother with quality? Because quality is critical for survival and success. The market for software is increasingly a global one, and your organization will not succeed in that market unless you produce, and are seen to produce, quality products and services. If you do not do so, your organization may not even survive. This is the first message of the chapter. It applies as much to software development and support as to any other product or service.

The word 'quality' means different things to different people. We give a formal definition later and discuss its implications, but in essence, quality means satisfying customers. A happy customer will do repeat business.

There are several reasons why you should be concerned with quality:

- quality is now a competitive issue;
- quality is essential for survival;
- quality is essential for international marketing;
- quality is cost-effective;
- quality retains customers and increases profits;
- quality is the hallmark of world-class businesses.

1.1.1   Quality is Now a Competitive Issue

Software used to be a technical business, in which functionality was the key determinant of success. Today, you can no longer rely on the functionality of your products to win the day. Your competitors can match your functionality relatively quickly and easily. The only way to differentiate your product from those of your competitors, beyond the short term, is by its quality, and the quality of support that goes with it.

As the software market matures, customers want to be assured of quality. They no longer accept your claims at face value, but expect you to demonstrate quality. Certification to international quality

3

standards is becoming a prerequisite for getting business; not to have certification will become a competitive disadvantage.

This applies to in-house information systems departments as well as to commercial software organizations. Internal customers also want quality assurance, and question increasingly whether work should be carried out in-house or outsourced by external suppliers.

1.1.2 Quality is Essential for Survival

Customers are demanding demonstrable quality. If you cannot deliver it, your ability to survive in a highly competitive and rapidly changing market is in doubt. More and more large organizations are deciding to reduce the number of suppliers they use, often by as much as 90%. In the drive to improve their own quality, they want to work closely with their chosen suppliers, whom they treat as business partners. They often use quality certification as a way of selecting suppliers.

1.1.3 Quality is Essential for International Marketing

The market for software is rapidly becoming global. The ability to demonstrate quality gives even a small company credibility to enter an export market.

The Single European Market came into being on 1 January 1993, and the European Economic Area Agreement (EEA) became effective in early 1993. The EEA countries (the European Community and seven EFTA states – Austria, Finland, Iceland, Liechtenstein, Norway, Sweden and Switzerland) represent the world's largest trading bloc, accounting for 40% of world trade, 30% of world production and 380m citizens. Government and multinational buyers in Europe are already using certification to internationally recognized standards as a criterion for shortlisting suppliers. Similar developments are taking place in other world regions – for instance the North American Free Trade Area (NAFTA).

It works both ways – your home market is vulnerable to quality foreign imports unless you can compete on quality.

1.1.4 Quality is Cost-effective

An effective quality system leads to increased productivity and permanently reduced costs, because it enables management to reduce defect correction costs by emphasizing prevention.

Everyone in the software industry knows that the cost of correcting defects in software late in development can be orders of magnitude greater than the cost of correcting them early. Preventing defects in the first place can save even more. It is possible to achieve this. Leading companies, such as IBM, are aiming at '6 Sigma' quality in the near future – a target of only three defects per million lines of code.

The scope for reducing costs can be demonstrated by applying the 'Cost of Poor Quality' technique. This is a way of analyzing business processes to identify targets for improvement initiatives. It is as applicable to a software organization as to any other business. It involves breaking the organization's costs into the following categories:

- **Basic** costs inherent in doing the work.
- The costs of low quality, comprising:
  - **prevention** costs, incurred to prevent defects from occurring, for example training, or corrective action aimed at eliminating the causes of failure
  - **appraisal** costs, incurred for example in testing software to ensure it meets requirements
  - **failure** costs, incurred in correcting defects found by appraisals, or by customers after delivery.

The costs of low quality can amount to more than 50 per cent of total costs in software organizations. Large savings can be made by analyzing these costs, and targeting resources to reduce them.

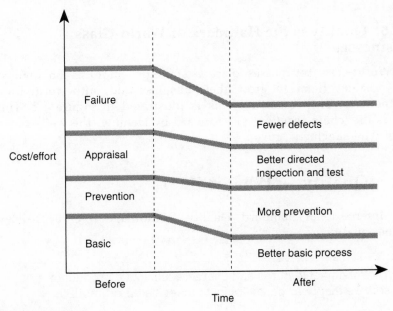

Figure 1.1 Costs of poor quality.

Typically this will be achieved by redirecting resources towards prevention. Introducing a quality system is an effective way to do this, as illustrated in Figure 1.1. This applies as much to in-house information systems departments as to commercial software organizations.

The initial costs of establishing a quality system are more than compensated for subsequently, and indeed significant returns can be achieved within one or two years. For example, Raytheon Equipment Division were able to reduce failure costs over a three year period from about 45% to 15%, and the cost of low quality by 20%, by improving their software engineering process.

Note that savings in the cost of low quality flow straight through to a firm's bottom line, and can dramatically increase profits!

1.1.5   Quality Retains Customers and Increases Profits

Poor quality often costs customers much more than it costs suppliers. Most customers will not tolerate this and will place their business elsewhere. Better quality leads to improved customer satisfaction, and increases the year-on-year retention of existing customers.

The sales cost of attracting a new customer is high. This gives customer retention a disproportionately large effect on profitability. A 1990 study by management consultants Gain & Co. showed that for software companies a 5% increase in customer retention increased profits by 35%.

1.1.6   Quality is the Hallmark of World-Class Businesses

World-class businesses place a strategic emphasis on quality. This enables them to grow their business and outperform their competitors. The reason for this is illustrated in Figure 1.2. This shows the 'chain reaction' put forward by Deming, the well-known quality management 'guru'.

1.2   Quality – What is it?

The International Standard Quality Vocabulary (ISO 8402–1986) defines quality as:

> The totality of features and characteristics of a product or service that bear on its ability to meet stated or implied needs.

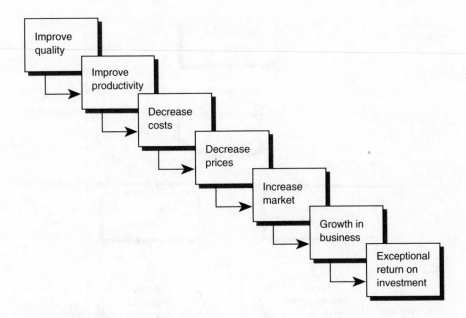

Figure 1.2 Deming's chain reaction.

Customers will be satisfied if their stated and implied needs are met, so this definition equates quality with customer satisfaction.

The customers' needs determine which features and characteristics are important for quality, and these will differ from case to case. Appendix C reproduces a general classification of characteristics relevant to software quality, taken from the international standard ISO 9126.

A software product displays quality to the extent that all aspects of the customer's needs are satisfied. This is determined by:

- how fully the need is understood and captured by a requirements definition;
- how well that definition is transformed into a software product;
- how well the product is supported.

This idea is illustrated in Figure 1.3.

To satisfy your customers consistently, you must build quality into the software process from requirements capture right through development and support of the product. You can then justly claim to be using a quality system.

1.2.1 Quality and Requirements Capture

The requirements capture process must identify and define the quality characteristics of a particular product that are critical for

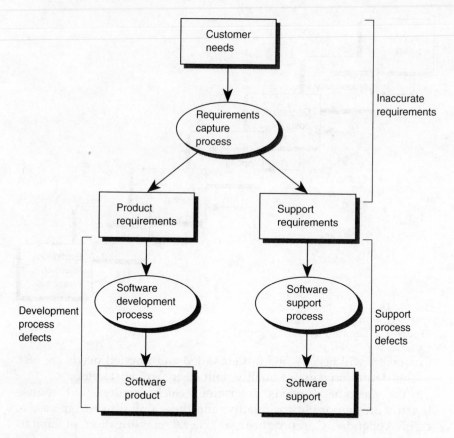

Figure 1.3 Sources of quality losses.

customer satisfaction, and distinguish them from the less important. For instance, in a particular case it may be critical that the software has suitable functionality, has very few bugs, and is easy to use, while efficiency is less important. This information will be used to assess and minimize the risks of not meeting requirements, guide design trade-offs during development and evaluate the acceptability of the product before it is delivered to the customer.

Some of these characteristics, such as functionality and correctness, are easy to define and test objectively. Others, such as usability, are harder to define and test because they are more subjective, being concerned with the standard of design and the 'feel' of the product. Yet subjective characteristics can be just as important as the objective ones. If the customers' subjective requirements are satisfied they will not merely accept that the product meets their needs, but enthuse about how well the product does the job.

The software developer's aim must be to achieve a level of quality that covers the subjective and objective components. This cannot be left to chance: subjective and objective needs must be identified and documented as measurable quality requirements. If this is not done, the developer will not be able to engineer them into the product.

Communication between the developer and the customer is the key issue. For bespoke software, the developer must work closely with the customer to develop and agree an accurate specification of quality requirements.

Where direct access to individual customers is not possible, for example in the high-volume packaged software market, the developer's marketing function must take the place of the customer, by taking responsibility for specifying market requirements. It is often appropriate to use prototyping and market research techniques to isolate and define the subjective quality characteristics. This may involve, for example, assembling a panel representative of the intended market.

The requirements capture process is often referred to as the analysis phase. It is extremely cost-effective to apply adequate resources to requirements analysis. Building the wrong product can be a very expensive mistake!

1.2.2   Quality and the Software Development Process

The software development process is the way in which the developer translates accurately stated requirements into software products.

It is clear that the quality of software is largely determined by the quality of the process used to develop and maintain it. This is no more than an extension of the principle that has been applied successfully in the manufacturing and service industries in recent years. It implies that to be successful software developers should focus as much on the software process as on the software product.

A good software development process must enable a software organization to deliver quality products consistently and economically. It is increasingly being recognized that it must do so in a timely way. Product cycle time is now a critical business issue for many developers. Software package vendors and the developers of various embedded software need to beat their competitors to the market with their products. Customers for bespoke software increasingly demand reduced development times to maximize their competitive advantage.

If these goals are to be achieved, the software development process should:

- use best software engineering practices;
- be supported where relevant by appropriate tools;

- be operated by appropriately trained and skilled staff, with clear responsibilities and instructions;
- emphasize defect prevention or early correction, rather than later detection and correction;
- generate records to demonstrate its effectiveness and efficiency;
- use such records to improve its performance in future.

One of the most influential advocates of the need to focus on process quality in the software industry has been the Software Engineering Institute, a federally funded research and development centre, affiliated with Carnegie Mellon University in the US. They have developed the Capability Maturity Model for software organizations, which is a five-level road map for improving the software process, based on the work of Watts Humphrey. An overview of this work is given in Appendix F.

1.2.3   Quality and Software Support

So far we have discussed quality in the context of developing software products, but it is vital for software developers to recognize that the quality of support for a product is normally as important to customers as the quality of the product itself. The software developer must make sure that the customers' support requirements are identified, and must design and engineer the business and technical environment from which the product will be supported. This applies equally to houses producing software packages or bespoke software and to in-house information systems organizations.

Support for software can be complex, and may include:

- user documentation, including on-line help text;
- packaging and distribution arrangements;
- implementation and customization services and/or consultancy;
- training;
- help desk assistance;
- error reporting and correction;
- enhancement.

For a bespoke application installed on a single site, the support requirement may be simply to provide a telephone and assign a staff member to receive and follow up queries.

For a major 'shrink-wrapped' product, it may mean providing localization and world-wide distribution facilities, and implementing major administrative computer systems to support global help-desk services.

1.2.4   What is a Quality System?

Applying the principles of quality to the software process is the beginning of success. The term 'quality system' is used internationally to describe a process which ensures and demonstrates the quality of the products and services it produces.

The ISO 9000 family of international standards define and describe what is required of a satisfactory quality system. ISO 9001 is the international standard for quality systems containing a design/development component. ISO 9000–3 gives guidelines for applying ISO 9001 to the development, supply and maintenance of software. ISO 9004–2 gives guidelines for services in general, which are applicable to software support services. Appendix A describes these standards in more detail.

Apart from ISO, many other industry, national and international bodies have promulgated standards which describe quality systems to be applied to software development and support in special circumstances. The most important ones are listed in Section 4.5, Alternatives to ISO 9000 Certification, with an indication of where they may be relevant.

The term 'quality management system' is sometimes used instead of 'quality system'. This emphasizes the need for the quality process to be actively managed to ensure that it continues to be effective and efficient when circumstances change. In particular, the standards of best practice are continuously evolving, and today's tools may not be appropriate tomorrow. Software developers must keep the practices and tools they use under review and make changes in a controlled way.

Just as important as the practices and tools are the staff who use them. The quality system must ensure that they have the right skills to do their jobs in a professional way. If they need training, they should receive it. It must also ensure that they understand their responsibilities and how their work relates to that of others.

Successful quality systems give great emphasis to early corrective action. It is much cheaper for the developer to correct errors early in the life cycle. It is also worth reflecting that an error might cost the customer much more than it costs the developer. The aim must be to ensure work is done 'right first time' at every stage of the development process. Quality control activities such as inspection and testing are therefore built in at every stage to detect errors as early as possible.

Better still is to avoid making errors in the first place. Successful quality systems include ways to analyze records of errors to determine their original causes and take action to prevent errors by eliminating their causes.

The quality system must assure customers and developers that software products developed under it will be of good quality. The quality system must be auditable. This means that the development process must be documented, and quality records, including suitable measurements, must be generated to demonstrate the achievement of quality and the effective operation of the quality system.

The overheads of such record-keeping need not be excessive if the quality system is carefully designed. The improvement in quality more than compensates for the costs involved.

The philosophy underpinning successful quality systems is that of continuous improvement of every aspect of the software process. The quality records and measurements are analyzed and used for this purpose. In the light of this analysis, senior management must regularly review the effectiveness and efficiency of the quality system, and ensure that action is taken to improve it.

In summary, a quality system is everything that management puts in place to ensure and demonstrate the quality of software products and associated support services. The quality system is the complete work process, including policies, procedures, tools and resources, both human and technological.

2
Managing a Quality Company

Quality is a journey which has milestones rather than a destination. It must be a continuing concern of a company's management, not something that is done once, then forgotten.

Managing a quality company is more than just implementing a quality system consisting of a set of techniques that meet ISO 9000 standards. It is the creation of a quality *culture* that permeates the entire organization.

This chapter deals with the nature of the culture that must be created in order to benefit from implementing the quality system described in Chapter 3. The culture change is noticeable when staff at all levels start to frown upon cutting corners and 'quick fixes', and go out of their way to help customers.

The characteristics of such a culture include:

- dedication to customer satisfaction;
- emphasis on continuous improvement;
- treating suppliers as business partners;
- communication and team work;
- empowering employees;
- commitment by top management.

2.1 Dedication to Customer Satisfaction

Quality is about customer satisfaction. Producing a quality product is an important part of ensuring customer satisfaction, but equally it is vital to give the same attention to customer care. This includes:

- putting enough effort into understanding customers' requirements, both for the product and its support;
- drawing up a contract that reflects these requirements;

- providing after-sales support to match customers' requirements or expectations;
- handling all contact with potential customers properly. First impressions count.

2.2   Emphasis on Continuous Improvement

The ultimate goal of 'total quality' will never be reached; it will always be possible to do things a little better, cheaper or faster. The real goal is to become a 'learning organization' that constantly draws on the resources and experience of all its staff to improve quality, reduce costs and respond faster to customers' needs. Having become a learning organization, learn how to learn *faster* than competitors. This requires constant emphasis on continuous improvement as a key value within the company culture.

2.3   Treating Suppliers as Business Partners

The quality of inputs to the software development process affects the quality of the end product. This is obviously the case for software purchased and incorporated in the final product, but it is also true of other inputs, such as software tools.

Rather than pressing suppliers exclusively on price and delivery which preserves an atmosphere of cut-throat competition, a quality approach means treating suppliers of key inputs as business partners. You expect them to provide excellent products and services, they expect and need you to pay a fair price. A close working relationship helps them to meet your needs better.

A step towards this is to require suppliers and subcontractors to demonstrate their quality by having the appropriate ISO certification.

This philosophy of business partnership can be extended to others with a stake in your business success. For instance, software houses producing software products for sale should consider whether their agents and distributors might be considered as business partners, to mutual benefit. And the same may apply to major customers, who are increasingly seeking such relationships.

Decisions on business partnerships are not taken for idealistic reasons, but are taken by business management in the light of strategic and commercial realities. They reflect the fact that business is not a 'zero sum game', and that it is often in your own interest to foster the success of others. In other words create 'win-win' situations.

2.4   Communication and Teamwork

Delivering quality to your customers depends on cooperation between many individuals or departments within your business (except in the smallest organization). This depends on excellent internal communications and teamwork.

The organization can be seen as a network of units supplying products and services to each other to enable the organization as a whole to satisfy external paying customers.

It is important to create a culture in which individuals and departments think of themselves as having their own customers within the organization. These internal suppliers then try to understand and meet the needs of their internal customers, and internal customers work with internal suppliers to help them do so. Responsibilities and lines of communication must be regularly reviewed, and traditional departmental relationships must be changed when they cease to be appropriate.

For instance, suppose the internal management information systems (MIS) department of a large firm discovers that it cannot meet its external customer's increasingly stringent availability requirements because there is no mechanism for its operations division to influence systems design in its early stages. An appropriate response could be to change the relationship between the systems design and operations departments, so that the operations department must specify operability requirements, and review and approve the design for operability before it is implemented (see Figure 2.1).

2.5   Empowering Employees

Staff will not be able to produce quality software and give quality support unless they have the necessary skills, knowledge and resources. Management must select the right staff for the job in the first place and must provide staff with the resources and training they need to give their best. This will motivate staff, and generate a commitment to excellence and continuous improvement. In these circumstances, authority and decision-making can be delegated to the appropriate level, where they can be exercised most effectively to respond promptly to customers' needs.

2.6   Commitment by Top Management

Quality cannot be simply delegated to a 'quality champion' or project leaders. While all managers and staff must own and take

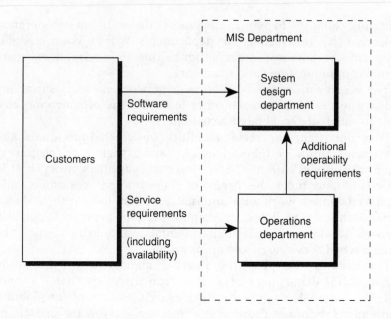

Figure 2.1 Interdepartmental relationships.

responsibility for day-to-day quality issues within their control, the quality endeavour must be supported, endorsed and enforced from the top, as part of the company culture. Attempts to improve quality without this will fail, since staff will feel unsupported.

By all means appoint a quality champion, but remember that the role of such a champion is to help top management fulfil their responsibility to quality. Top management can best fulfil this responsibility by:

- treating quality as a strategic business issue;
- developing a policy for quality;
- ensuring the quality policy is communicated and implemented throughout the organization;
- regularly reviewing the policy and its implementation.

2.7   Total Quality Management

The approach to management of a company described in this chapter is often known as Total Quality Management (TQM). It encourages management to give as much attention to the quality culture of the organization as to its management and technical systems. This is because:

> Quality programmes that fail do so for one of two reasons, they have passion without systems or systems without passion.
>
> (Tom Peters, Thriving on Chaos.)

3
Implementing a Quality System

How can we achieve quality? Many years ago John Ruskin gave us a pointer when he said that quality is never an accident, it is always the result of intelligent effort. Ruskin's remarks were made during a more leisurely age, but they still apply. For modern business, intelligent effort must be directed through a quality system.

3.1   Towards a Quality System

A quality improvement programme leading to the establishment of a quality system must have both technical and cultural aspects, each being equally important. It is easy to see the reason for this: the entity to be improved consists of both technology *and* people.

3.1.1   Technical

This involves developing standards and procedures to implement quality in all activities. The best software engineering practices should be used for the technical activities of software development and support, but attention should also be given to the non-technical activities that support them, such as marketing/sales, purchasing, personnel and finance. It also involves selecting and implementing the methods and tools necessary to support best practices, and training staff to use them. It establishes an infrastructure in which quality can be achieved.

3.1.2   Cultural

Quality must be accepted by everyone as the company's central value, otherwise the technical programme is of no use. Each person must be aware of a personal responsibility for quality. A key feature of the quality improvement programme is that it should involve everyone. A lively and appealing education programme must be established to achieve this involvement.

Another vital feature of a quality improvement programme is that it should be never-ending. The organization's environment is always changing – customers' or market needs, technology, personnel, competitors and their capability. The quality system must be kept under regular review to ensure that it continues to be effective, efficient and appropriate to the organization's environment and needs. When reviews show changes are needed, another cycle of quality improvement must begin.

The way small organizations implement a quality system will differ in detail from that of larger firms, and each will use different levels of resources, but the principal steps are the same for all (see Figure 3.1).

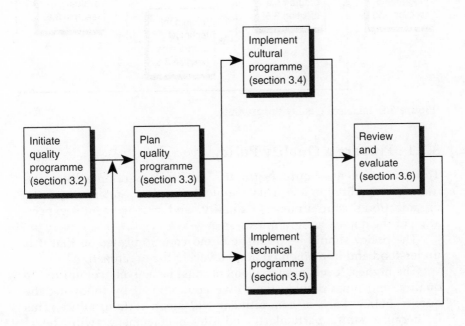

Figure 3.1 Steps to establish a Quality System.

3.2   Initiate a Quality Programme

The steps involved in initiating a quality programme are described below (see Figure 3.2).

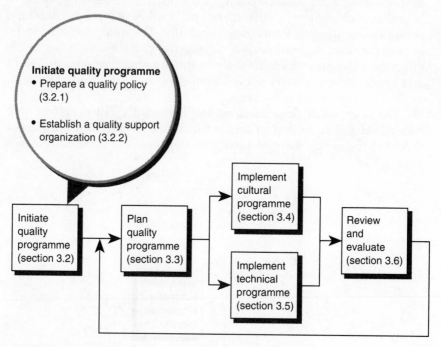

Figure 3.2 Initiate a Quality Programme.

3.2.1   Prepare a Quality Policy

Top management should begin the quality programme by form-ulating a quality policy. This should be a clear statement of the organization's commitment to quality, and management's expect-ation of the quality programme.

The policy should be published, and communicated so that it is understood and implemented at all levels in the organization.

The highest levels of management must be actively committed to quality, and must display their own commitment by following the quality policy. Lack of commitment will mean certain failure. This is because staff, particularly middle management, will detect management's attitudes, and will respond to the priorities they perceive to be set.

Top management is more accustomed to analyzing business issues in terms of costs, rather than quality. It is often important to make the link between quality and costs explicit, to generate the level of commitment required. Top management can use the 'cost of poor quality' technique in Section 1.1.4 (Quality is Cost-effective) to very good effect at this point, to overcome residual doubts about the business case for quality.

The quality policy will underpin the implementation of the quality system. It is vital from the start that it is communicated to all staff so that they know what to expect and why, and are in no doubt about management's firm commitment to quality management.

3.2.2 Establish a Quality Support Organization

Since a quality programme is a sizeable task it requires a support organization, which must operate in the company mainstream and involve management and staff drawn from across the whole organization. Any other approach allows people to remain outside the quality programme and claim that quality is someone else's responsibility.

The quality support organization normally comprises a steering committee and a quality improvement team (QIT). Senior company management must be on the steering committee. The committee's task is to oversee the quality programme.

The main functions of the steering committee are:

- to set the strategic direction and longer term goals;
- to establish a quality improvement team, and review its performance;
- to authorize and approve a budget for the quality programme;
- to provide high-level support for the quality programme.

Early in the process, the steering committee should set up a QIT whose main functions are to establish and sustain the quality programme throughout the organization. Specific activities will include:

- assessing the organization's needs;
- designing the quality system to meet them;
- planning and monitoring its implementation.

Other quality programme activities will be spread throughout the organization, but the QIT may also be involved in:

- communicating the programme to staff;
- training and other activities in support of the cultural programme;
- preparing and reviewing procedures and standards;

- selecting methods and tools;
- establishing a programme to measure the software process, products and services.

A senior manager, ideally an experienced software engineer, should lead the QIT and champion the cause of quality within the organization. Quality champions will be among the first to be formally trained in quality principles. They will be expected to guide the QIT through the early stages of the quality programme.

It is also important to train formally every other member of the QIT in quality principles, as soon as possible, because a well-motivated QIT will be the driving force of the whole quality programme.

In larger organizations, one or more members of the QIT may work full-time on the quality programme. In smaller organizations, QIT membership will probably be a part-time role, and the steering committee and the QIT might be a single group. In the smallest organizations the QIT will probably be most or all of the staff.

No matter what form the quality support organization takes, top management must drive it. They are the 'customer' for the quality system, which the QIT will establish under the quality champion's leadership. They must review each step of the quality programme to ensure it meets the business needs of the organization. The quality champion must have a clear, direct line to top management, irrespective of his or her level in the organization, and must seek their involvement and approval at each step.

When a quality support organization is in place, the quality programme can be planned in detail.

3.3   Plan a Quality Programme

The steps involved in planning a quality programme are described below (see Figure 3.3).

3.3.1   Assess the Organization

Most organizations have areas of good practice and areas of bad practice. The first task of the QIT is to find out where these strengths and weaknesses are. This is done by measuring current practice against an appropriate yardstick of good practice. The organization should select the yardstick that best meets its needs from a number of alternatives.

ISO 9000 Standards

A 'baseline audit' is carried out to measure current practice against the requirements of ISO 9001 and its guidelines – ISO 9000–3 for software, and ISO 9004–2 for support services. The audit examines the organization's activities under various headings, including those shown below.

Management Responsibility for Quality	Quality Planning
	Maintenance and Support
Quality System Documentation	Configuration Management
Contract Review	Change Control
Project Control	Document Control
Design Control	Quality Records
Process Control	Purchasing
Verification, Validation and Testing	Internal Quality Audits
	Training
Corrective Action	

ISO 9000 standards are applicable to all sizes and types of organization at this stage of a quality programme, and are likely to be the default choice unless there are strong reasons for choosing another yardstick.

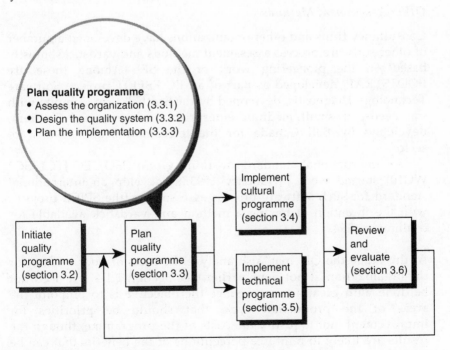

Figure 3.3 Plan a Quality Programme.

The SEI's CMM

A Software Process Assessment is carried out against the Capability Maturity Model developed by the Software Engineering Institute (SEI). See Appendix F for details. This yardstick is widely used in the US, particularly by contractors of the US Department of Defense which commissioned its development and uses it for evaluating the capability of their suppliers in procurement. It is less likely to be appropriate outside this environment, or for any but the largest developers.

Part 2 of This Book

Part 2 of this book can also be used to compare your current practice with what is recognized today as the best software engineering practice. It has been strongly influenced by the European Space Administration's Software Engineering Standards (PSS–05), which have been through a number of versions and represent the accumulated experience of many thousands of software engineers. If you implement effectively the practices designated in Part 2 as **essential**, ISO 9000-3 requirements will be satisfied. (In some respects, the practices described exceed the requirements of the standard.)

Other Assessment Methods

Consultancy firms and other organizations have developed a number of other software process assessment methods and yardsticks, mostly based on the pioneering work of the SEI. Among these are BOOTSTRAP, developed as part of an EC ESPRIT project, Software Technology Diagnostic, developed by the Scottish firm Compita with the needs of small/medium enterprises in mind, and Trillium, developed by Bell Canada for the telecommunications software sector.

An international standards working group (ISO/IEC JTC1/SC7 WG10) started work in January 1993 to develop an international standard for such software process assessments (the SPICE project), with the intention of having a method and yardstick available for trialling in 1994.

At this stage the QIT may also analyze the costs of poor quality for the organization, if not done earlier (see Section 1.1.4). It need not be done with great accuracy, since the objective is to pinpoint the areas of the production cycle that should be priorities for improvement, not to justify the costs of the programme, though the results are likely to reinforce perceptions of the benefits that can be gained.

Many firms will find it useful to employ a software quality management consultant during this and possibly subsequent phases of the quality programme. It can be valuable to have an experienced outsider carry out the assessment activity and 'hold up a mirror' to the organization. A suitably qualified consultant ideally should have a solid background in software development, together with practical experience in the design and implementation of software quality programmes. Before appointing a consultant, you should verify their experience, in particular by following up references, and then prepare and agree a carefully considered brief on your aims and objectives.

3.3.2 Design the Quality System

When the quality assessment is complete and its results have been analyzed, the objectives of the company-wide quality system should be defined. These are analogous to a 'requirements specification' for the quality system. The QIT led by the quality champion will normally help to develop the objectives, which will be based on the key areas revealed by the quality assessment. But top management are the 'customer' for the organization's quality system. They must formally approve the objectives, and ensure they are consistent with business needs. In particular, they must ensure the objectives are consistent with any other initiatives being taken within the organization – conflicting objectives between quality and other initiatives can only damage both.

Objectives should be expressed in measurable terms where possible, so that they are clear and precise. This not only allows the QIT to make trade-offs in designing the quality system, but makes it easier to align them to business objectives.

Typical objectives are:

- Reduce the number of faults found in testing and operation.
- Improve productivity.
- Reduce development timescales.
- Improve responsiveness to customer requests.
- Improve accuracy of estimating and scheduling.
- Achieve ISO 9001 certification.

Having agreed the objectives the QIT can then design the quality system in outline. This design should be documented in the quality manual.

The quality manual is a document which summarizes how the organization's overall quality system works. It should be short; 20 pages would be sufficient. Its central purpose is to describe:

- What must be done.
- Who is to do it.
- When it is to be done.
- How it is to be done.

The quality manual will be used as a design specification while the quality system is being established, but it will have many other valuable uses. Once the quality system has been established, the quality manual becomes the top level of reference for anyone who wants to know how the organization does its business. It will be used by new entrants to the organization as an aid to induction. It may be shown to customers, to give them confidence in the organization's capability. It will be used by auditors from independent certification bodies, if such certification is sought.

Typically the quality manual will contain:

- The organization's quality policy and objectives.
- An organization structure showing the duties and responsibilities of all those who manage, perform and verify work affecting quality.
- A description of the life cycle model (see Section 3.5.1).
- An overview of the quality system.
- The relationship of the quality system with ISO 9000.
- Reference to detailed procedures and standards (see Section 3.5.2).

The development of the quality manual is an important learning process for the organization, helping the quality system meet the organization's needs. Organizations may be tempted to buy in a ready-made quality manual developed for another organization – several consultancy firms offer such manuals. Such a ready-made quality manual is unlikely to meet the organization's needs without significant changes, because each organization and its circumstances are unique. They should be viewed with great caution, though access to sample manuals can be useful.

The first version of the quality manual will undoubtedly be amended during the implementation of the quality system, as the QIT gains greater understanding of the organization's needs. The manual must be subject to strict document control. This means setting up procedures for:

- Proper approval and distribution.
- Keeping records of authorized holders of the document.
- Reissuing documents after a predetermined number of changes.
- Withdrawing obsolete versions.

The quality manual should be reviewed against an appropriate yardstick, usually the requirements of ISO 9001 and the 9000–3 and 9004–2 guidelines, and receive formal approval, normally from the chief executive. Any subsequent issues must be approved by the same authority.

3.3.3   Plan the Implementation of the Quality Programme

When the first version of the quality manual is complete, the QIT can determine the amount of work needed to implement the quality system and make appropriate plans.

Introducing a quality system is a complex task both organizationally and technically, needing the same level of planning and control as a major software development project.

The QIT must develop a comprehensive project plan detailing schedules, activities, milestones, deliverables and required resources for the implementation of the quality system. Since the project will involve the entire organization, the QIT must keep everyone informed from the earliest planning stages.

Typical tasks to be undertaken are:

- Implementing a cultural programme.
- Adopting a life cycle model.
- Designing a document control system.
- Developing and documenting procedures and standards for every activity and deliverable of each life cycle phase.
- Developing and documenting procedures and standards for support activities.
- Defining and implementing a measurement programme.
- Reviewing and, if necessary, revising the quality manual.
- Quality appreciation and quality system training.
- A quality audit programme.
- Management reviews.
- ISO 9000 assessment.

The timescales for the quality programme will depend very much on the size of the organization, and the state of development of its quality and software engineering practices. Quality improvement is a never-ending, cyclical process, and the quality programme will conclude with a review activity, which will launch the next cycle.

The time taken to achieve ISO 9000 certification is likely to be between nine and eighteen months, including three to six months to build up records demonstrating the effectiveness of the quality system. Many organizations will prioritize the actions required to achieve certification, and go through more than one iteration of the plan/implement/review loop.

3.4 Implement the Cultural Programme

For a quality programme to succeed it needs the support of the whole organization. To win that support, a carefully planned cultural programme must be implemented early in the quality programme (see Figure 3.4).

The cultural programme has three principal aims:

• Generate awareness of quality.
• Encourage participation by everyone.
• Ensure ownership.

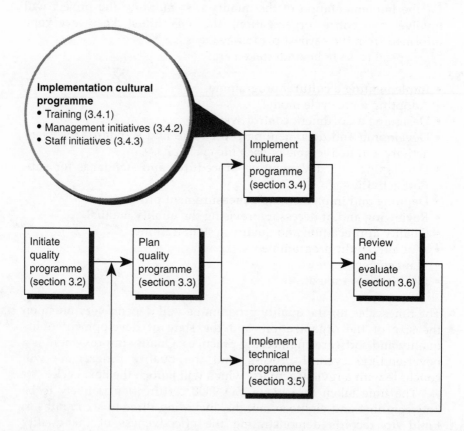

Figure 3.4 Implement the Cultural Programme.

To achieve these aims, the initiatives and techniques described below should be considered. They fall into three categories:

- Training.
- Management initiatives.
- Staff initiatives.

Organizations (particularly small ones) should be careful not to start too many initiatives together, in case they lose focus and reduce the effectiveness of the programme.

3.4.1 Training

Quality Appreciation Training for Managers and Staff

All staff must be introduced to the principles of quality including the 'costs of low quality' (see Section 1.1.4). This is vital in all sizes of organization. It is discussed in detail in Section 3.5.5.

Quality Workshops

These provide opportunities for all staff to discuss company-wide quality issues. Quality workshops are useful in all sizes of organization.

3.4.2 Management Initiatives

Goal Setting

This gives each staff member measurable quality objectives, which should be agreed rather than imposed. This can conveniently be done as part of regular staff performance appraisal.

Analysis of Defects and Their Causes

This technique teaches the principle that a defect is not properly corrected until its cause has been discovered and action has been taken to prevent its recurrence. It should be carried out systematically in all parts of the organization by the staff who do the work. This is extremely valuable in all sizes of organization.

A useful description of how such a technique has been applied in IBM is given in *Experiences with Defect Prevention* (IBM Systems Journal, Mays *et al.*, **29** (1) 1990).

Department Purpose Analysis

This is a powerful technique, for use in larger organizations, that can involve large numbers of staff in the quality programme. It is undertaken by a team of staff in each department to:

- Clearly define the purpose of the department and align it with business strategy and goals.
- Clearly define the requirements of the department's internal and external customers, and the working relationships that exist between them and the department.
- Carry out an activity/task analysis of the department to determine what is being done and why.
- Decide whether each activity/task adds value or is a cost of poor quality.
- Identify improvement projects and prioritize them for action.

3.4.3 Staff Initiatives

These initiatives rely primarily on the voluntary contributions of staff, but they also need to be fostered and supported by management.

Suggestion Schemes

These are a formal means of gathering quality improvement suggestions from all staff. There should also be ways of giving recognition to staff who make valuable suggestions; not necessarily financial.

All suggestions must be followed up and their proposers told whether their suggestion has been accepted or not, and the reasons why. Nothing is more likely to demotivate staff than a feeling that management is ignoring them.

Quality Circles

Quality circles allow people to suggest quality improvements in their own areas. They are widely used with great success in Japan. An extremely clear overview of their use in Nippon Electric Company (NEC) is given in the paper *Software Quality Improvement* by Yukio Mizuno, *IEEE Computer*, March 1983 (Mizuno, 1983).

3.5 Implement the Technical Programme

The steps involved in implementing a technical programme are described below (see Figure 3.5).

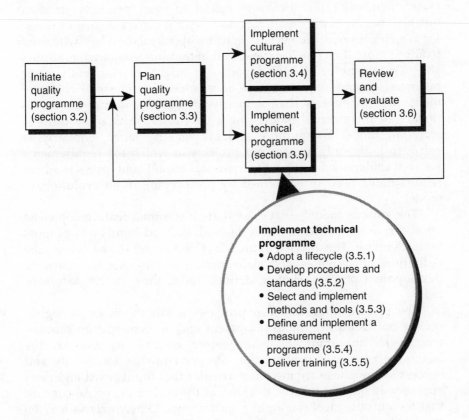

Figure 3.5 Implement the Technical Programme.

3.5.1 Adopt a Life Cycle

Before an organization can develop a comprehensive set of standards and procedures, it must have a clear, agreed view of how it should develop software.

This view is best provided through a life cycle model. All software development organizations, large or small, should adopt one. Many different kinds of life cycle model have been developed to meet the needs of particular circumstances. The chief kinds, described in more detail in Section 6.2, are:

- Waterfall.
- Incremental.
- Evolutionary, or spiral.

The organization will need to select the most appropriate type of life cycle, then tailor the life cycle model to meet precisely its own business needs. Many organizations carry out different sorts of work, for which different life cycles might be appropriate. They will need to adopt more than one life cycle, and determine when each is applicable. For example, an MIS department might develop both major business systems requiring tens of man-years, and small enhancement jobs taking less than a man-year. For the former an evolutionary or incremental model might be chosen, with some form of waterfall model being more suitable for the latter. Similarly, a software house might carry out projects in which the requirements are well understood using an incremental model, and projects where requirements need to be refined by prototyping in an evolutionary model.

The various models that exist share a common feature: a phased approach to the software life cycle, with defined inputs and outputs for each phase. This phased approach is important, since it allows the definition of activities and deliverables making up the software development process. Having defined them, they can be documented.

The phased approach also provides a minimum set of logical review points during the development and implementation process, which are important for management control. Reviews at the beginning of phases confirm that the prerequisites for quality and success of the phase are met: in particular that inputs exist and meet appropriate quality criteria. Reviews at the end of the phase confirm that the outputs meet the input requirements. Other reviews may be specified within each phase. Such reviews form an essential part of the quality system.

3.5.2   Develop Procedures and Standards

Many software development organizations operate with the highest standards and procedures, but in many cases few of them are written down.

It is common for software developers to resist written standards and procedures, using a variety of arguments to justify their attitude. They are too bureaucratic, or unduly constrain creativity or are too much of an overhead. These arguments must not be rejected out of hand if they are made by capable staff, because the wrong standards and procedures blindly imposed can be very damaging. Nevertheless, the right procedures and standards, written down, are immensely valuable to the organization, and an essential ingredient of a quality system. They represent the lessons the organization has learned on how best to build quality software. They are the necessary basis for continuous improvement in the future. They also facilitate the movement of staff between projects and the training of new staff.

Procedures should be written describing how each activity must be carried out, with standards describing what each deliverable should look like. They must be easily accessible to the people who need them. They need not be on paper – electronic procedures and standards are quite acceptable, provided they are subject to proper control. They must be formally reviewed to ensure they are appropriate, and formally approved by management before being used. The managers of the areas in which they will operate should normally do this, since they are responsible for seeing that they are followed.

Procedures and standards are the second level of quality documentation, below the quality manual, and referenced from it. Like the quality manual, they must be subject to strict document control (see Section 3.3.2).

Procedures and standards must provide an adequate level of control over the software development process, be concise, easy to understand and usable. At minimum, they must ensure that staff following them meet the requirements of the appropriate ISO 9000 standards. This does not mean that every tiny detail must be written down. Intelligent, well-trained and highly skilled staff should be expected to work within sensible high-level constraints. If your standards and procedures are too detailed, they are unlikely to be used in practice, and will not achieve the desired result. Remember that they will be reviewed regularly and may be elaborated upon if necessary. Apply this question as a test: 'Will absence of this detail affect quality?'

There are many sources of pre-existing standards and procedures: other organizations or consultants, national standards, international standards and industry standards (for example the comprehensive IEEE standards). Whatever sources are drawn on, some degree of tailoring will be needed, if only to capture lessons learned by the organization in the past. Developing a comprehensive set of standards and procedures is a major task for most organizations. The workload should be spread widely to involve the greatest possible number of people. This will increase the level of support for the quality system and help foster a spirit of ownership.

The software engineering practices defined in Part 2 of this book can be used as a specification for the new standards and procedures that are needed at this stage.

It is important to ensure that new procedures and standards are developed and reviewed by their users and those affected by them. This helps to ensure they are relevant and workable. Failure to do this could result in their being unusable.

New standards and procedures must be introduced sensitively and gradually. It is wise to test them on a pilot project before introducing them more widely.

3.5.3 Select and Implement Methods and Tools

Among the most critical components of any software quality system are the 'methodologies' (methods) used, both to develop products and to manage the development process. Tools that implement the methods are also important, and may be critical. For instance, it can be very difficult to implement adequate configuration management for a complex product, without suitable automated support systems. It can also be difficult to keep documentation for integrated business application systems up to date on paper, without data dictionary / repository tools.

The choice of methods and tools is important, not just for their immediate impact on the organization's capability, but for the way they can constrain its longer term development. In other words, methods and tools – software engineering – are a strategic issue. It is appropriate for top management to review the organization's current portfolio of methods and tools, develop a vision of the kinds of methods and tools it will need to employ in the future (say 3–5 years' time) to meet its business objectives, and plan the transition from one to the other.

This book gives broad guidance on how to select and implement appropriate methods and tools. It does not recommend specific ones, which would be impossible in general. What suits one software development organization may not suit another. The nature of the software to be produced and the hardware / software platforms on which they run also influence the choice.

Strategic Considerations

Tools in themselves do not substitute for a disciplined management approach to quality. They will not solve underlying problems of organization and unsatisfactory practice. Good practice should dictate which tools to use, not vice versa.

It is unwise to attempt too many changes together, and it is easier to implement new tools and methods successfully if basic project and configuration management disciplines are already in place. You should therefore consider carefully whether the time is right to introduce new tools and methods.

Methods and tools may be equally important for support activities such as estimation, project management, configuration management, and problem management as for life cycle activities such as analysis, design, construction and testing.

The more complex the software product, the more critical tool support is likely to be. Use of the right methods and tools can give competitive advantage. The wrong methods and tools may be a disadvantage.

The Computer Aided Software Engineering (CASE) market-place is developing very rapidly. Many software developers are looking to CASE tools to make dramatic improvements in productivity and reliability in the near future.

Specification, Evaluation and Selection

It is important to specify clearly your objectives and your requirement of a method or tool. Without these, you are unlikely to reap the benefits you expect.

Several directories of tools and associated methods are published in Europe and North America, some of them on-line databases. They can be very useful and cost-effective in shortlisting candidate tools. Other useful sources of information are specialist software engineering newsletters and trade exhibitions.

Integration of tools is an increasingly important issue. Any new tool must work successfully with other tools in use or being acquired.

If you want to be a quality provider, you must purchase from quality suppliers. The quality of support may be as important as functionality when you select a tool. How responsive would a potential supplier be to problem reports? Is the user documentation adequate? Is training available? What about future enhancement plans?

Be aware that the choice of tools can lock you into a proprietary environment, which may be rendered obsolete by changing technology.

If no suitable tool can be found, it may be sensible to develop one in-house. A bespoke tool may help you compete; but consider the lifetime costs of developing, supporting, and enhancing it.

Implementation

Careful planning is required to bring new methods and tools into use successfully and to achieve the desired benefits.

It is wise to use a new method or tool on a pilot project, before bringing it into company-wide use.

Consider carefully the training needed by staff to use new methods and tools effectively.

Consider setting up a scheme for process and/or product measurements to determine whether new methods and tools are achieving your objectives.

Reviews

Plan to review new methods and tools after their implementation to determine whether your objectives have been met, and, if not, decide what to do about it.

Plan to review the portfolio of methods and tools in use and the overall software engineering strategy, and adjust strategy and plans as required. These reviews should take place regularly, say every one or two years. The CASE market-place moves rapidly and new products or approaches may be more suitable.

3.5.4   Define and Implement a Measurement Programme

It has rightly been said that 'if you can't measure it, you can't manage it'. A measurement programme provides essential feedback, which steers process improvement. The measurements must be defined, collected, analyzed, reported and acted upon. They will include measurements of software products, services, and process.

When defining what should be measured it is important to be very clear about why it is required, and what it will be used for. A badly chosen set of measurements can be expensive to collect and impossible to analyze and act upon. An approach known as GQM (standing for Goal, Question, Measurement) is often used to ensure this. With GQM, the starting point is a goal the organization wishes to achieve, for instance: G1 – *improve project productivity*. The next step is to identify questions, answers to which will determine whether the goal has been met. In this case they might be: Q1.1: *how much code is written?* Q1.2: *how much is reused?* and Q1.3: *how much effort is lost in rework?* The final step is to identify measurements that will answer the questions. These could be: M1: *lines of code per person -month.* M2: *% components reused.* M3: *% effort in rework.* This is illustrated in Figure 3.6.

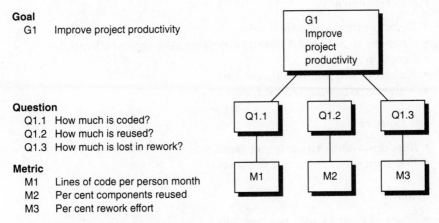

Goal
G1   Improve project productivity

Question
Q1.1 How much is coded?
Q1.2 How much is reused?
Q1.3 How much is lost in rework?

Metric
M1   Lines of code per person month
M2   Per cent components reused
M3   Per cent rework effort

Figure 3.6 Goal, Question, Measurement.

The measurements chosen should:

- Closely reflect customers' requirements or process attributes which directly bear on those requirements: quality cannot be improved by optimizing against a measurement which does not relate to a customer need.
- Be clearly defined, so that all those collecting and using the measurements are using the same definitions.
- Not take undue trouble and expense to collect and analyze: a few relatively crude measurements that are inexpensive to collect but taken consistently, so that they yield comparative results, may be more useful than a complex expensive scheme. It is worth considering whether tools can be used to collect data automatically and help with analysis.

Measurements can be used at both the project and the process levels for many different purposes, for example:

- At the project level, to identify unusual components for more detailed study (those that are unusually error-prone, for example).
- At the process level, to calibrate an estimating model.
- At the process level, to compare the use of different methods and tools on different projects.
- At the process level, to monitor progress towards improvement goals.

Each organization must define what measurements to take, how to take them, and how to use them to meet its own particular needs, but the following represents a minimum set of attributes that should be included:

For development

- Defect counts and defect rates.
- Changes to approved requirements and design specifications.
- Productivity.
- Adherence to planned timescales.
- Adherence to planned budget.

For support

- Responsiveness to customer requests.
- Frequencies of customer requests.

General

- Costs of poor quality (see Section 1.1.4).

3.5.5   Deliver Training

The success of the quality system will depend ultimately on the skill and commitment of the people operating it. For this reason comprehensive training at all levels is an essential ingredient of a quality programme.

Three types of training are required:

- Quality awareness training.
- Quality system training.
- Job skills.

Quality Awareness Training

Quality awareness training should be provided to everyone in the organization as part of the cultural programme (see Section 3.4). It should be designed to ensure that each person accepts their own responsibility for quality. It should emphasize that everyone, no matter what their position in the organization, has customers – internal or external – whom they should continually try to satisfy.

Such training can be bought in from training companies or consultants, but it is often more effective and cheaper in larger organizations to use an internal, cascaded team learning approach, such as that recommended by consultants in Total Quality Management. In such an approach the 'top team' is trained initially by an external consultant, then each member of the top team trains the team they lead, and so on through the organization. Specially trained 'facilitators' are often used to advise the line trainers. One benefit of this cascaded approach is that it can help to overcome resistance to change from middle management; nothing is more calculated to increase personal commitment to an idea than having to train others in it! Another benefit is the focus on team learning. Every team within the organization participates in a quality workshop, which is focused on the concrete realities of their shared goals.

Quality System Training

Quality system training is of two types: general and specialist.

General. Each person should be trained thoroughly to fulfil their part in the operation of the system. This means being aware of the standards and procedures that apply to their own jobs, competent to implement them and understanding how they fit into the overall system. This training is typically delivered on the job or in short seminars by supervisors or other in-house staff.

Quality specialist training. Some staff will have specialized roles within the system and will require appropriate specialist training.

The 'quality champion' and members of the QIT will need training in ISO 9000 principles. (This will have been given at the very start of the programme, but is included here for completeness.)

Staff who will carry out audits of the system will need training in quality auditing (see Section 3.6.2).

Some larger organizations, which implement departmental systems, may find it useful to train a small number of staff in software process assessment. The form of assessment will depend on the companies' needs (see Section 3.3.1), but could be ISO 9000 assessment, or assessment to the SEI's Capability Maturity Model, or some other approach. These staff will contribute to management review by conducting in-depth assessments of departmental systems.

Some organizations with very mature systems will use statistical process control (SPC) techniques to monitor and control quality levels. Such techniques are used in 'cleanroom engineering' for instance. Staff responsible for such activities will need training in SPC.

Job Skills

Managers should identify the training needs of each staff member to ensure that appropriate training is provided as part of a planned programme in which the skills learned are quickly used. Training without consolidation on the job is often ineffective. Personal training plans should be reviewed as part of formal performance appraisal arrangements. Such training falls into the following categories.

Management skills. Project management skills are crucial to software development, and appropriate training for project managers is very important. Other general management training is also important.

Personal effectiveness. Training should also focus on the development of personal effectiveness skills, such as:

• Time management.
• Problem solving.
• Communication skills.

Technical skills. It is essential that software development staff have the necessary training in the methods and tools they are to use.

The organization must establish mechanisms for training needs to be reviewed regularly and also when staff move between jobs. Records of the training and experience of individual members of staff must be kept to allow this to be done. The initial cause of particular quality problems is often inadequate training or experience.

3.6 Review and Evaluate

A quality system is dynamic, and must be allowed to develop in line with changing circumstances. This means that each component of the system must be reviewed regularly, and action taken to ensure its continued effectiveness (see Figure 3.7). The components to be reviewed include the organization structure and responsibilities, procedures and standards, methods and tools, and resources (including staff and their training). Changes should be made as soon as necessary.

Techniques that help ensure that the quality system continues to reflect the true needs of the organization include:

• Project reviews.
• Quality audits.
• Management reviews.
• Follow-up.

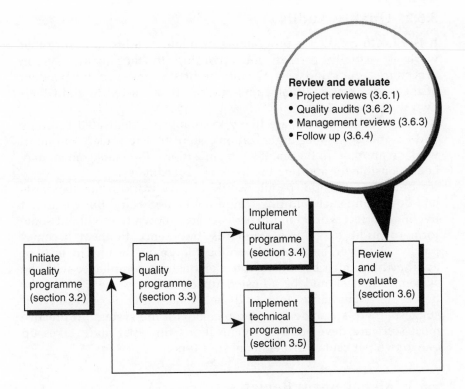

Figure 3.7 Review and Evaluate.

3.6.1 Project Reviews

All projects, whether successful or not, should be reviewed on completion to determine what lessons can be learned, and how to embed them in the quality system.

This is so obviously a good thing, yet so often not done, that some explanation is required. The reluctance to carry out project reviews is perhaps due to a psychological need for 'closure' once a task has been completed. The individuals concerned want to move on to the next thing, and the last thing they want to do is to relive the pains of the last project, particularly any aspects that were unsuccessful!

Post-implementation review should be a phase in the standard project life cycle – but senior management follow-up will be necessary to ensure they take place.

3.6.2 Quality Audits

It is vital to conduct a programme of quality audits to ensure that work is actually carried out according to the quality system procedures and standards. Quality audit staff must be independent of the work they audit, since no-one can be expected to audit their own work objectively.

Large organizations are likely to establish a dedicated full-time audit team. In smaller organizations, staff on one project can audit work on another. In the smallest organizations, top management may be responsible for auditing the work of subordinates.

In a perfect world, people would always work to the standards laid down, and such auditing would not be necessary. But we do not live in a perfect world, and experience has shown that without some form of audit to enforce standards, adherence to them becomes patchy. However, audit should not be a large overhead. The level of audit activity must be sufficient to demonstrate compliance with the system, but it should be adjusted up or down in the light of the degree of compliance found. If heavy auditing is necessary, it suggests there are underlying problems with the system. In practice most software development organizations find that audit takes up one to two per cent of professional staff time.

3.6.3 Management Reviews

Since top management has the ultimate responsibility for the effective operation of the quality system, it must review the system regularly, at least annually, to ensure that it is operated properly and that it remains suitable and effective. These reviews should draw upon all relevant sources of information including:

- Results of audits, internal and external.
- Project review reports.
- Customer service reports.
- Technology changes.
- Customers' assessments of service quality.
- Analysis of measurements.

The result of the management review will be a list of actions required to maintain and improve the system. This is the input to the planning phase of the next cycle of quality improvement, which continues in an unending plan/implement/review loop.

This process of management review ensures that the quality system can adapt to a rapidly changing environment. It institutionalizes continuous improvement, a hallmark of successful, world-class companies.

3.6.4   Follow-Up

It is very important to record the results of project reviews, quality audits and management reviews, and follow up any actions arising from them. This ensures that the agreed actions have been taken, and are having the desired results.

4
Quality Certification

To recap: quality is critical for survival and success. A prerequisite for it is an effective, economical quality system, and we have seen in Chapter 3 how to establish one. In this chapter we examine how the software developer can recognize an acceptable quality system, and demonstrate its achievement to customers.

4.1 What is ISO 9000 Certification?

Certification of a quality system follows an independent assessment which demonstrates that it is effective. It provides evidence that the organization is capable of producing quality products and services, but it does not, and cannot directly evaluate the quality of any particular product or service. Three things are needed for certification:

- A suitable yardstick.
- A means of assessing against the yardstick.
- Industry-wide recognition of both the yardstick and the assessment mechanism.

Happily, there are schemes that satisfy these requirements.

ISO 9000 certification is the most important of these for most software organizations. The international standards ISO 9001, ISO 9000–3 and ISO 9004–2 provide an internationally recognized yardstick, a specification of the minimum requirements of any acceptable software quality system (see Appendix A for details). Several external bodies, which are recognized as objective across the industry, provide independent assessment against the international standards, and publicly register firms that pass the assessment. Section 4.3 explains what ISO 9000 certification involves from the point of view of an organization seeking it. Section 4.4 outlines what arrangements have been put in place for it around the world.

There are alternatives to ISO 9000 certification. These are discussed in Section 4.5.

44

Software products can be certified against relevant standards by an independent party, just as quality systems can. This is of real importance in some markets, for instance certified compliance with Open Systems Interconnection (OSI) standards for communications software. Arrangements for product certification are less well developed than those for quality system certification at present, but product certification can be expected to become more usual in future.

Pointers to the future include: plans to establish a scheme to certify accounting packages in the UK; and an initiative to set up a European network to carry out independent software product assessments using the methodology developed by the ESPRIT SCOPE project.

The remainder of this chapter will consider only quality system certification and not software product certification.

4.2 Reasons for ISO 9000 Certification

There are two main reasons why software developers should seek ISO 9000 certification:

- To gain competitive advantage.
- To set an objective target for a quality programme.

These reasons apply to different firms in varying degrees, but most, if not all, software developers will decide to seek certification. The market for software is global, with strong international competition in all countries. It is worth reflecting on the vision put forward by the TickIT software quality initiative in the UK, which is that by 1999:

> The top 5000 firms in Europe will have ISO 9001 certification for their in-house software quality systems
>
> All bid-lists will demand ISO 9001 certification

4.2.1 Competitive Advantage

Increasingly, multinationals and public sector organizations require their software suppliers to be certified against ISO 9000 standards if they are to be included in bid-lists. This trend, particularly evident in Europe, intensified in the run-up to the Single European Market in January 1994. In December 1989, the Council of the European

Communities adopted the international standards as the basis for a European policy on conformity assessment. In the near future, not to be certified will be a competitive disadvantage.

There are also marketing advantages to be gained from being listed in public registers used by buyers, and from use of associated certification marks in advertising and promotional literature.

In-house software developers, although not directly competing on the open market, are increasingly asked to justify their costs against third party vendors. Certification helps them to compete on equal terms. They may also use it to assure their internal customers of the quality of their products and services. As more firms seek certification for supply of their non-software products and services, they will increasingly demand such assurance from their internal software suppliers.

4.2.2 Objective Target for a Quality Programme

Top management of organizations that have begun a quality programme must set targets that are objectively testable. Certification of the quality system to ISO 9000 provides a very clear, objective target against which progress of the programme can be measured.

The cost of ISO 9000 certification is not excessive. It depends on such factors as the size of the firm and the number of sites, but will always be small compared with the up-front costs of establishing a quality system in the first place, and smaller still compared with the benefits it will yield. For instance, the main component of the charges made by a certification body will relate to the number of man-days used at experienced consultant rates: to certify a software developer with 200 professional staff will take of the order of 10–15 man-days; smaller firms will need less.

Achieving the target of certification also provides recognition for employees, and raises morale throughout the firm.

4.3　What ISO 9000 Certification Involves

This section examines what certification involves in general terms. Section 4.4 outlines how to obtain more information about services available in different countries.

4.3.1　Selecting a Certification Body

When a firm has decided to seek ISO 9000 certification, it must then select which certification body to use.

In most countries, there are several bodies that provide ISO 9000 certification services, though not all of them are active in the software industry. A number of bodies can provide certification services internationally.

Among the factors that should be taken into account in selection are:

Reputability

There is no benefit in obtaining certification from a body that lacks a good reputation for standards of assessment. The European Commission has been fostering the harmonization of standards of assessment, and mutual recognition of certification in readiness for the Single European Market after 1992. To do this, they have adopted a series of standards (EN 45000 series) for the accreditation of certification bodies. Accreditation certifies a body as competent to conduct certification, and gives evidence of reputability. Accreditation arrangements are not yet fully in place across Europe, so that there are at present reputable European bodies that are not accredited. Other countries outside Europe where accreditation is being actively pursued include the US, Australia, New Zealand and Japan.

Acceptability of Certificate

Firms should be careful to choose a certification body whose certificate is recognized and acceptable in its target markets. They should confirm that there is mutual recognition of the certificate with reputable bodies in their target markets.

Relationships With Other Firms

Large firms, particularly multinationals, often wish to seek certification separately for their operating divisions or subsidiaries. At the same time, they may want to maintain a degree of central control, so as to build a strong working relationship with a single certification body, and to negotiate certification costs centrally.

Costs

Different certification bodies levy different charges for their services, and large firms may be able to negotiate reduced charges, depending on the volume of their business. Certification bodies compete with each other, and it is sensible to invite tenders from several firms. However, take full account of the factors previously discussed before making a decision, which should not be based on price alone.

4.3.2   Use of Standards in Certification

When a firm seeks certification against ISO 9000, the certification body determines which standards in the series are applicable. The decision is based on the description of business activities for which the firm applies for certification (this is known as the 'scope' of certification). Firms may apply for certification for just a part of their business, and this facility is often used to advantage by firms wishing, for whatever reason, to move by stages to a fully certified quality system.

The business activities of most firms in the software industry (using the term in the broadest sense) are a mixture of providing software products and associated support services in various ratios. Firms providing 'pure' software products are extremely rare; invariably customers require at least an error-correction service. On the other hand, firms providing 'pure' software-related services do exist, for example consultancy, training, distribution and retailing firms. Most firms lie somewhere in between.

All firms applying for a scope that involves any development and/or maintenance and enhancement of software will be assessed against ISO 9001 (because design is necessarily involved), using the ISO 9000-3 guidelines. ISO 9004-2 service guidelines will also be used for those parts of the scope involving support for software products over and above basic maintenance and enhancement (which are covered by ISO 9000-3).

A service firm applying for a scope that does not involve development, maintenance or enhancement of software will also be assessed against ISO 9001, using the ISO 9004-2 guidelines, if the service it provides involves a non-trivial design component. This would apply for instance to a consultancy firm that recommends or configures hardware and software from other suppliers to meet business requirements. It would also apply to a firm providing bespoke support services tailored to individual customers' needs.

If the services within the scope do not involve design, or it is trivial, ISO 9002 may be used as the assessment standard, using the ISO 9004-2 guidelines. This would apply to many consultancy, training and service bureau firms. The test is whether the design input offers scope for failing to meet customer requirements: if it does, ISO 9001 is required. Simplicity of design indicates simplicity of assessment, it does not mean design can be ignored. An example of trivial design for which ISO 9002 is appropriate could be deciding the route of cable ducting. If you are in any doubt as to which standard is appropriate, you should clarify it with your chosen certification body.

4.3.3 The Certification Process

The details of the certification process depend on the procedures adopted by the chosen certification body, but there are common features.

The firm should first establish its quality system (see Chapter 3). Most firms will wish to obtain an assessment of their current practice against ISO 9001 by a consultant, or an in-house expert. If this is done at the start of the quality programme, the firm will be able to decide what must be done, how long it will take and how much it will cost, and the consultant will be able to advise on selection of the certification body and how it operates.

The firm makes a formal application to the certification body. This is normally on a standard form provided by the body, which includes details of the firm's business and the scope of certification sought. A copy of the quality manual may also be requested at this stage. Many certification bodies are struggling to keep pace with the demand for their services, so it is sensible to apply well in advance of the date you expect to be ready for certification.

The certification body will normally make a preliminary visit in order to find out more about the firm, explain the certification process, and agree costs and timescales.

In the first stage of the assessment proper, the certification body assesses whether the quality system documentation, including the quality manual and procedures and standards, complies with ISO 9000 requirements. The firm will be advised of any deficiencies, which must be put right before proceeding further.

In the second stage of the assessment, the certification body sends a team to the firm's premises to audit practice against the defined quality system and ISO 9000 requirements. Any discrepancies found are reported to the firm for correction. The assessment can have three outcomes:

- Unqualified pass with no discrepancies (this is almost unheard of).
- Qualified pass with minor discrepancies that must be corrected within an agreed timescale before certification.
- Failure. Discrepancies found are either so major, or so numerous though minor, as to demonstrate a complete breakdown of the quality system. In this case the firm must reapply when the deficiencies have been corrected.

In the case of a qualified pass, the audit team make a follow-up visit to the firm at an agreed time to confirm that corrective action has been taken and has been effective.

The firm is then registered as certified. The details of the firm and its certified scope are entered on a public register maintained by the certification body. The certification body will normally supply copies of a certificate, which many firms choose to display in prominent positions on their premises, such as entrance lobbies. Often the firm is also licensed to use a special mark belonging to the certification body on its advertising material, letterheads and other promotional material, though this must not be used to imply certification of any product: it is after all the quality system that has been certified, not the product.

Thereafter the certification body pays regular surveillance visits to the firm, to ensure that the quality system continues to be effective. The frequency of these is determined by the certification body, which normally reserves the right to make unannounced visits, though in practice some warning is given to ensure that appropriate staff are available. Some assessment bodies make a practice of carrying out a full assessment audit after a certain period, in addition to the lower-key surveillance audits.

4.4   ISO 9000 Certification around the World

4.4.1   ISO 9000 Certification Outside the Software Industry

The growth in demand for ISO 9000 certification outside the software industry has been explosive since 1987, when the standard was first introduced – close to a doubling every year in many countries. Different countries are at different points of an exponential growth curve. Europe is generally in the lead, and the UK within Europe (no doubt because the international standard is a development of an earlier British Standard). It is difficult to determine the exact number of certified companies in each country, since there is no pan-European register and there are many certification bodies, both state sponsored and commercial, but a survey in 1992 by NSAI, the Irish standards and certification body, produced the results in Table 4.1.

Interest in certification outside Europe is generally less, but is growing fast due to a perception that, in many industries, it may become necessary for success in the European market. There is already strong interest in certification in such countries as Canada,

Australia and New Zealand, and increasingly the US and the emerging Asian economies.

Table 4.1 ISO 9000 Certified Companies, 1992.

United Kingdom	13,500	Switzerland	370	Spain	100
Ireland	500	Germany	400	Others	100
France	495	Italy	250		

4.4.2   A Global Overview of ISO 9000 Certification for Software

The software industry has come relatively late to ISO 9000, but there are signs that the demand for certification by software firms will grow at least as fast as that for other industries. The main drivers are major government and multinational purchasers (to qualify suppliers for inclusion on bid-lists) and suppliers (for their own competitive advantage).

In the light of this rapidly growing demand, it is not surprising that arrangements for certification are developing rapidly across the world. Particular issues are:

Competition. In many parts of the world, including Europe, a competitive market in certification services is a public policy objective. In these circumstances, several certification bodies compete for business, rather than a single national body carrying out all certification. Such a fast-growing business is attractive to commercially minded firms. A number of certification bodies, both public and private sector, are emerging as international players, able to meet the certification needs of multinational companies.

Equalization of standards. Certification is of no value unless there is general confidence that all certified firms meet a common standard, whether assessed by the same or different certification bodies. This is achieved by a process of accreditation (see Appendix A.6), whereby an accreditation body assesses, and in effect 'certifies', the competence of certification bodies to operate to common standards. As of early 1993, accreditation was not widely in place, but a number of countries were working toward it, many using the influential UK TickIT scheme as a model (see Section 4.4.3).

Mutual recognition. Confidence in certification within a country can be established by a nationally administered accreditation scheme, such as TickIT. Similar arrangements with a common accreditation are conceivable within a region or some other grouping. But accreditation alone does not address genuine confidence in certificates across the global software market, between groups with a common accreditation. For instance, how can a purchaser know if a US or Japanese certificate is equivalent to a UK certificate? There is no prospect at present of a single global accreditation authority. This issue is a long way from being resolved. Individual certification bodies are concluding mutual recognition agreements, but perhaps the best hope for the future would be mutual recognition agreements at the level of accreditation bodies.

The following sections give a snap-shot of the situation in different countries and regions as it appeared in early 1993. Firms should either seek advice from a suitable consultant, or research the current and likely future position in their own country and major markets, before making decisions on certification bodies and schemes. Useful contact points include:

National accreditation bodies. Accreditation bodies certify certification bodies as competent. Many countries are in the process of setting them up, but few are yet in place. They are an authoritative source of information on reputable certification bodies active locally, and the industrial scopes for which they are competent.

National quality associations. Most countries have one or more independent membership organizations that promote quality across the board. They sometimes operate their own quality registration schemes, as does the Irish Quality Association with its high-profile Quality Mark scheme, adapted from ISO 9000.

National standards bodies. The national representative to the International Standards Organization. Note that a division of the national standards organization often acts as a certification body, so their advice may not be strictly independent.

Other bodies. These include trade associations, national informatics societies, and in some countries, organizations set up specifically to promote software quality.

4.4.3   UK and TickIT

The ISO 9000 standards were based, in part, on the 1975 version of British Standard BS 5750. Individual standards in the ISO 9000 series are still published in the UK as parts of BS 5750 (ISO 9001 equates to BS 5750 Part 1 and so on), and are still frequently known by their BS 5750 part number. This is giving way to the ISO number, and the trend should be encouraged, since it causes less confusion in increasingly global markets.

Quality system certification has had a long history in the UK, but the certification bodies concerned were mainly purchasers, acting in 'second party' mode, and accreditation did not exist prior to 1985.

In 1987 the UK government commissioned two complementary

studies of the relevance of ISO 9001 to software. These arrived at similar conclusions:

- All the quality system standards in common use were similar, and ISO 9000 was the best route for harmonization.
- Action was required to improve market confidence in third party certification, and there was an urgent need to establish an accredited certification body or bodies for the software sector.
- Authoritative guidance material was required to assist those implementing quality systems to relate generic ISO 9001 requirements to the software industry, and to facilitate common interpretation by auditors.
- Professional practice amongst software quality system auditors needed to be improved.

As a result, a new, more uniform accreditation scheme was set up to extend certification to the software field. This is known as TickIT. It is described in detail in a book commonly referred to as the *TickIT Guide* (Guide to Software Quality Management System Construction and Certification using EN 29001) (DTI, 1992), which is also a very useful reference book for any organization implementing an ISO 9001 compliant quality system. The main features of the scheme are:

- Certification bodies are accredited to carry out TickIT certifications by the National Accreditation Council for Certification Bodies (NACCB), using EN 45012 criteria. To be accredited they must meet the following 'uniform accreditation arrangements':
  - use the TickIT name and logo (see Figure 4.1) only in connection with accredited certification. When the TickIT logo is used on certificates it must be accompanied by the certification body's mark and the NACCB logo.
  - evaluate applicants management review activities annually as part of surveillance
  - mutually recognize TickIT certifications issued by other TickIT accredited certification bodies
  - use TickIT guidance documentation in the *'TickIT Guide'*. This includes ISO 9000–3, and a guide for auditors. The latter is the European IT Quality System Auditor Guide which has been adopted for use throughout Europe as part of ITQS, an EC supported European 'Agreement group' (see 4.4.4)
  - use only TickIT auditors entered on the UK National Register for Assessors of Quality Systems maintained by the Institute of Quality Assurance (IQA).
- To be TickIT registered, auditors must:
  - have successfully completed a five day TickIT registered auditor

training course, substantiated by an examination, and
- demonstrate their technical competence, proficiency and integrity at an interview by a joint professional panel of the IQA and the British Computer Society.

The TickIT scheme has proved successful and is now well established. The first certificates under the scheme were issued in mid 1991. By the end of 1993:

- More than 300 organizations had been certified, including many outside the UK, from elsewhere in Europe, and from Japan, India and Brazil.
- Six certification bodies had been accredited (BSI Quality Assurance, Bureau Veritas Quality International Ltd, Det Norske Veritas Quality Assurance, Lloyd's Register Quality Assurance, SGS Yarsley Quality Assured Firms and BMT), and two others were seeking it.
- Ninety two individuals had been registered as TickIT auditors (the vetting process is rigorous: 15% of applications fail paper scrutiny, and 25% fail at interview).

Figure 4.1 TickIT logo.

4.4.4 Europe

Many certification bodies are active certifying software quality systems across Europe. Accreditation bodies have been set up in some countries, for instance NACCB in the UK, and RvC in the Netherlands. However, arrangements for accreditation and mutual recognition of certificates are confused and fluid.

The Commission of the EC, EFTA, CEN, and CENELEC established a body called the European Organization for Testing and Certification (EOTC) in April 1990. The purpose of this body is to encourage, foster and manage the development of European certification systems and mutual recognition agreements. The EOTC infrastructure consists of *Sectoral Committees*, representing manufacturers, users, consumers and third parties, and *Agreement Groups*, comprising testing and certification bodies prepared to sign and manage mutual recognition agreements.

A number of agreement groups have been established, but these overlap and compete:

- E-Q-Net is composed of the national leading 'not for profit' certification bodies associated with the national standards bodies of 14 European countries. Some 50 bilateral recognition agreements had been signed between E-Q-Net members by late 1992. These do not specifically apply to certification of software quality systems.
- The European Committee for Quality System Assessment and Certification, known as EQS, had made little progress by late 1992.
- The group known as ITQS (Recognition Arrangement for Assessment and Certification of Quality Systems in the Information Technology Sector) is specifically concerned with certification of IT quality systems. It has adopted the European IT Quality System Auditor Guide used in the UK TickIT scheme. ITQS offers mutual recognition of IT sector certificates between its members, and maintains a central register of certificates. However, as of late 1992 many large, reputable certification bodies were not members of ITQS. One TickIT accredited certification body was a member, but not others, although TickIT certificates are mutually recognized!
- The Independent International Organisation for Certification (IIOC). IIOC members will not issue ISO 9000 certificates based on audits by other organizations. IIOC also advocates mutual recognition agreements between accreditation authorities on a worldwide basis.

The certification bodies appear to be jockeying for position in a way which can only damage the confidence of industry in ISO 9000 certification if it continues. It is very desirable that compatible schemes for accreditation and mutual recognition of software quality system certificates be established across Europe in the near future. If this happens, it will probably be derived from the UK TickIT scheme.

4.4.5   North America

US

Interest in certification of quality systems to ISO 9001 has grown considerably in the US from a very low level as at 1990. Several certification bodies are active, including European firms, some of which are TickIT accredited and offer TickIT certificates.

The Registrar Accreditation Board (RAB) and the American National Standards Institute jointly operate the American National Program for Registrars of Quality Systems. The RAB formed a Software Quality Systems Registration (SQSR) committee in October 1992 to assess the need for a sector scheme for software quality systems registration, using the TickIT Guide as the base document. It looked likely in early 1993 that a scheme compatible with TickIT would result, meeting the test of mutual recognition between ANSI-RAB and the UK NACCB, and other EC accreditation bodies. It has been agreed with ITQS for example that the US will not unilaterally change the European IT Quality Auditor Guide, but will input comments to the ITQS change control mechanism. In late 1993 firm proposals for the SQSR scheme were being considered by the RAB Operational Council. They have generated considerable debate, and some sections of the US software industry have expressed concerns about the initiative.

Canada

In Canada the Quality Management Institute, a subsidiary of the Canadian Standards Association, has been certifying quality systems since 1979. Initially the standard used was CSA Z299, one of the contributing standards to the ISO 9000 series. Few countries except the UK have such extensive experience with quality system certification.

There is also interest in the TickIT accreditation model. An industry grouping, chaired by the Canadian Information Processing Society at the invitation of the Canadian Standards Association, concluded that TickIT could meet the requirements of the Canadian software industry. In early 1993 the intention was to develop an action plan that responds to Canadian needs and takes into consideration Canada's federal/provincial jurisdictions.

4.4.6 Pacific Rim

Australia and New Zealand

Certification to ISO 9000 is used extensively in manufacturing and many service industries, and several certification bodies are active. It is promoted by governments through quality oriented purchasing policies.

In the software area, the picture is complicated by the existence of Australian standard AS3563 – Standard for Software Quality Management Systems. Many people consider this a superior standard to ISO 9000–3, and it was accepted as an IEEE standard in late 1992. It is used in Australia as a compliance standard in place of ISO 9001 (AS3901), rather than as guidelines in support of ISO 9001, though in practice a quality system conforming to either standard is likely to conform to the other. Many local firms have been certified against AS3563. Some firms, typically larger with an eye to export markets, have been certified against ISO 9001 for software, either alone or as a dual certificate with AS3563. Most state governments regard use of either standard as acceptable for software suppliers.

The Joint Accreditation Scheme – Australia and New Zealand (JAS–ANZ) was set up in 1992 to accredit certification bodies. JAS–ANZ procedures require use of trained auditors who have been certified by the Quality Society of Australasia (QSA). JAS–ANZ policy is to adopt international standards or guides for accreditation, where they are available. JAS–ANZ has held preliminary discussions with accreditation bodies operating in the UK (NACCB), the Netherlands (RvC) and the US (RAB), with a view to developing mutual recognition.

Japan

There has historically been some resistance to the idea of ISO 9000 certification in Japan, but this appears to be changing. With the 40-year history of quality management in Japan, certification in the Japanese software industry can be expected to spread very rapidly once accreditation and certification arrangements have been put in place.

- The ISO 9000 series were adopted as Japanese standards in October 1991, and were published as the JIS Z9900 series.

- As of September 1992 the JMI Institute was undertaking certification in the fields of machinery and electrical and electronic industry based on a memorandum of understanding with BSI-QA. There was no Japanese body certifying software quality systems, but a foreign company was undertaking TickIT certification. The Japanese Standards Association Quality Audit and Inspection (JSAQAI) intended to operate as a certification body and train auditors, with a coverage including software.
- The Japan Federation of Economic Organizations (Keidanren) established the Japan Accreditation Board for Quality System Registration (JAB) on 1 November, 1993. It is a non-governmental, non-profitmaking foundation funded by many industrial sectors, with governmental authorization by the Ministry of Trade and Industry and the Ministry of Transport. By March 1994 a number of certification bodies were pursuing accreditation, but none had yet been accredited.
- A JAB committee is discussing certification in the software industry, and was expected to publish a concluding report in April 1994.

Korea

The ISO 9000 series were adopted as Korean standards in April 1992. Although there were no arrangements for ISO 9000 certification in Korea, by mid 1992 there was some interest in setting them up. The Information Technology Standardization division of the National Computerization Agency is actively studying the requirements for a scheme for certifying software quality systems.

Singapore

The Singapore Institute of Standards and Industrial Research (SISIR) and the National Computer Board (NCB) jointly launched an ISO 9000 IT Certification Scheme in October 1992. Under this scheme SISIR certifies quality systems covering software services and products.

SISIR has signed mutual recognition agreements with leading overseas certification bodies in Europe, North America and Australasia. As of early 1993, these did not explicitly cover software certification, but the IT Certification Scheme was looking at accreditation with other internationally recognized schemes such as TickIT in the UK.

The NCB has established a software quality improvement programme to help local companies set up quality systems and work towards ISO 9000 certification.

4.5   Alternatives to ISO 9000

ISO 9000 certification is not the only form of assessment that can yield the benefits quoted in Section 4.2: gaining competitive advantage, and setting an objective target for a quality programme. Other approaches will be more suited to the specific circumstances of some organizations, although ISO 9000 certification is likely to be preferred by most, at least in the early stages of quality improvement.

4.5.1 SEI Maturity Assessment

The Capability Maturity Model (CMM) was developed by the Software Engineering Institute (SEI) for the US Department of Defense, based on the pioneering work on software process improvement by Watts Humphrey; see his excellent book *Managing the Software Process* (Humphrey, 1989). The SEI have developed two methodologies for using the CMM: Software Process Assessment (SPA), for use by a software organization with the objective of improving its own processes (possibly with the assistance of an external consultant); and Capability Evaluation (CE), for use by a software procurer (or a third party agent of the procurer) to evaluate the risks associated with potential suppliers' processes for a particular contract. The SEI provide training in SPA for those organizations wanting to carry out self-assessments. They have also trained and licensed a number of commercial vendors to carry out third party assessments. The CMM itself is a public domain document.

The CMM characterizes five levels of increasing process maturity, from Level 1 'Initial' or 'Ad Hoc' to Level 5 'Optimized', by the extent to which the organization's processes comply with specified key practices. An overview of the CMM is given in Appendix F.

Organizations can use the maturity model to assess the maturity of their current process. They may then use it to specify a goal for process improvement (for instance, 'we will achieve maturity level 3 in 15 months'), and if they wish have an assessment carried out by a vendor licensed by the SEI, to confirm objectively that they have achieved the goal. A number of US software developers have taken this approach with considerable success. For example see the paper *Software Process Improvement at Hughes Aircraft* by Watts Humphrey, Terry Snyder and Ronald Willis in IEEE Software, July 1991. A number of self-help groups called Software Process Improvement Networks (SPIN groups) have grown up in the US to support individuals in companies seeking to improve their processes. The SEI serves as a hub to keep these groups in touch.

Note that the SEI maturity approach applies only to software developers, unlike ISO 9000 and the TQM awards, which can be used to drive a quality programme throughout an organization whose business is only part software.

A number of criticisms have been made of the SEI maturity approach. First, it reflects the business needs of large organizations working in the US defense software sector, and it is difficult for smaller firms outside this sector to apply it. Secondly, it 'hardwires' within it a particular order for improvement actions, which may not be appropriate in all circumstances.

There is considerable debate about where in the SEI scale of maturity ISO 9001 compliance lies. Most observers would probably say that it lies somewhere between level 2 and 3, though it is possible to devise scenarios where an ISO 9000-compliant firm is at level 1. This means that it is possible for organizations who are already certified to ISO 9001 to use the SEI approach to set more challenging improvement goals.

Firms who are involved in the US defense software sector should probably use the SEI maturity approach rather than ISO 9001, because it is proven in that community. In any case, they are likely to be subject to capability evaluation by the DOD when they bid for contracts, and need to align their own processes to the CMM which underpins it.

The CMM should also be considered as a driver for further improvement by larger organizations in other sectors with relatively well developed quality systems, those which have already achieved ISO 9000 for instance. A number of large telecommunications multi-nationals are using it.

At present smaller organizations, and those with relatively undeveloped quality systems, would probably do better to use ISO 9000.

4.5.2 Total Quality Management Award Schemes

The total quality management (TQM) movement has spawned a number of national and international awards to give public recognition to total quality and business excellence. The criteria for the awards can also be used as a yardstick for assessment and as an objective target to drive improvement. They are framed in general terms, and can be employed in all commercially trading sectors of industry, including software. In keeping with their TQM origin, they measure a much broader range of features relating to quality than ISO 9000 or the SEI's CMM. They are just as concerned with human resources and cultural issues, and with quality and business results, as they are with quality system and process. Because of this breadth, they are an attractive supplement to ISO 9000 for companies with well developed quality systems who wish to drive further cycles of process improvement after achieving ISO 9000 certification. In this sense they may also be an alternative to the SEI's CMM, particularly for companies for whom software is only a part of their business. Success in winning an award can be a useful marketing tool, but most companies will not win an award, and participation in itself confers no competitive advantage. The best-known award schemes are:

- Malcolm Baldrige Award (US).
- European Quality Award.
- Deming Award (Japan).

Malcolm Baldrige Award

The Malcolm Baldrige National Quality Award is an annual award to recognize US companies with excellent quality management and quality achievement. The award criteria and measurement framework are adjusted (improved) each year – the details given below are for the 1992 scheme. They are built upon these core values and concepts:

- Customer driven quality.
- Leadership.
- Continuous improvement.
- Full participation.
- Fast response.
- Design quality and prevention.
- Long-range outlook.
- Management by fact.
- Partnership development.
- Public responsibility.

The core values and concepts are embodied in seven measurement categories, with associated maximum marks, as follows:

- Leadership (90).
- Information and Analysis (80).
- Strategic Quality Planning (60).
- Human Resource Development and Management (150).
- Management of Process Quality (140).
- Quality and Operational Results (180).
- Customer Focus and Satisfaction (300).

The framework connecting and integrating the categories is given in Figure 4.2. It has four basic elements:

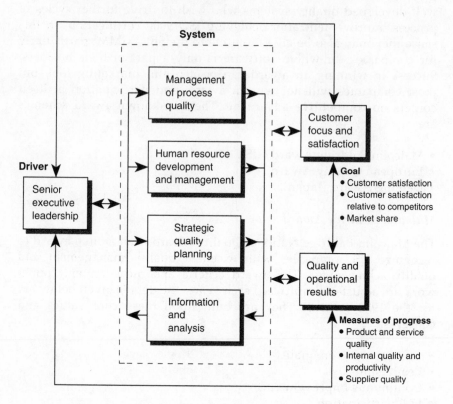

Figure 4.2   Baldrige award criteria framework.

Driver. Senior executive leadership creates the values, goals and systems, and guides the sustained pursuit of quality and performance objectives.

System. Comprises a set of well-defined and well-designed processes for meeting the company's quality and performance requirements.

Measures of Progress. Provide a results-oriented basis for channelling actions to deliver ever-improving customer value and company performance.

Goal. The basic aim of the quality process is the delivery of ever-improving value to customers.

This framework and corresponding marks illustrate well the breadth of coverage of a TQM award compared to ISO 9001. Most of the ISO 9001 criteria fall into the category labelled Management of Process

Quality, with small contributions to other categories. It is unlikely that ISO 9001 compliance on its own could contribute more than a quarter of the maximum 1000 marks.

European Quality Award

The European Quality Award is administered by the European Foundation for Quality Management with the support of the European Commission and the European Organization for Quality.

Figure 4.3 illustrates the assessment model and marking scheme underlying the award, which may also be used for self-assessment. Processes are the means by which the company harnesses and releases the talents of its people to produce results. In other words the processes and the people are enablers which provide the results. *Customer satisfaction, people (employee) satisfaction* and *impact on society* are achieved through *leadership* driving *policy and strategy, people management, resources* and *processes,* leading ultimately to excellence in *business results.*

Deming Award

This award is presented annually in Japan. Historically, it was the first of the TQM awards to be established – the Malcolm Baldrige Award and the European Quality Award are modelled on it. It is named after W. Edwards Deming, the US quality management pioneer who worked in Japan for much of his career.

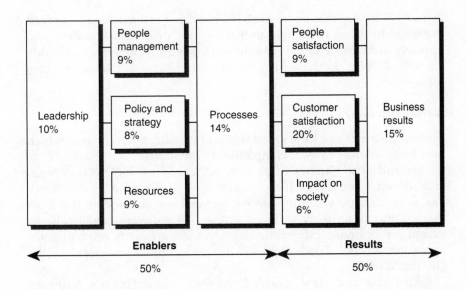

Figure 4.3   European quality award assessment model.

4.5.3   Other Schemes

Schemes Deriving from the SEI's CMM

A number of proprietary assessment methods are available, all influenced by the SEI, which can be valuable alternatives as supplements to ISO 9001:

- BOOTSTRAP, developed as part of an EC ESPRIT project,
- Software Technology Diagnostic, developed by the Scottish firm Compita with the needs of small/medium enterprises in mind,
- Trillium, developed by Bell Canada for the telecommunications software sector.

An international standards working group (ISO/IEC JTC1/SC7 WG10) started work in January 1993 to develop an international standard for such software process assessments (the SPICE project), with the intention of having a method and yardstick available for trialling in 1994. It is intended that this will:

- draw on the best features of existing assessment schemes, in particular the CMM;
- be compatible with ISO 9000;
- recognize explicitly organizations' business needs;
- be applicable by organizations of all sizes, in all sectors.

If the SPICE project is successful, the resulting international standard promises to be an extremely useful tool for process assessment and improvement. More details of this work are given in *Software Quality Journal*, **2** (4), 1993, which is dedicated to software process assessment.

National schemes

Some countries have local standards and certification schemes, which may be of interest to local companies. For instance:

Ireland. The Quality Mark scheme, based on ISO 9000 criteria, and administered by the Irish Quality Association. The Quality Mark has a very high visibility among general consumers in the Irish market, but is unlikely to be of interest to software organizations, except for in-house information systems departments of companies operating in the Irish domestic market themselves seeking the Quality Mark.

Australia and New Zealand. AS3563 – Standard for Software Quality Management Systems. Many people consider this a superior

Part 2

Software Engineer's Guide
To Best Practice

Part 1 of this book identified the importance of quality; the need to develop a quality culture and implement a quality system throughout the organization, based on the best current software engineering practices. Part 2 examines in more detail these practices and the principles on which they are based.

Chapter 5 outlines the quality, management and engineering principles that are the basis for the practices of the subsequent chapters. It also gives an overview of the framework into which these practices have been structured. It describes the purpose and structure of the framework and gives guidance on how it can be applied in a particular organization.

Chapter 6 deals with life cycle activities. That is, the activities concerned with the analysis, design, development, installation and maintenance of a software product to satisfy a user need. The chapter covers these activities in a way that does not presume the use of any specific life cycle models, development methodologies or tools.

Chapter 7 is concerned with the organizational and technical management of the life cycle activities. These are referred to as the supporting activities and cover the following areas:

- Project management.
- Configuration management.
- Verification and validation.
- Quality assurance.

The activities covered by Chapters 6 and 7 are essentially project level activities. They are carried out independently at project level. Chapter 8 looks at activities at an organizational level. These are required to ensure that project level activities are carried out to a consistently high standard. It includes activities such as management of the software process, procurement of inputs to the software process, training and the responsibility of management with respect to documenting its policy, objectives and commitment to quality.

5
Applying Best Practice to Projects

5.1   Software Engineering Definition

Software engineering is defined in the IEEE glossary of software terminology (IEEE, 1993) as:

> The application of a systematic, disciplined, quantifiable approach to the development, operation and maintenance of software.

It is significant that the definition refers not merely to the development of software, but also to its operation, maintenance and retirement. These activities form a major part of the life cycle of a software product, but are often viewed as being less important than development. It is important to bear in mind that a software product is developed to satisfy a customer need. The need will not be static, but will evolve over the lifetime of the product. The lifetime is ultimately determined by the software's ability to evolve effectively.

From a customer's point of view, operations and maintenance are the most important part of the software's life cycle. The environment for effective and efficient software maintenance and support must therefore be as rigorously designed and engineered as the product itself.

The development of consistently high quality software and service support requires that the software process used to develop these products and services be based on sound software engineering principles incorporating current best software engineering practices. The following section overviews the principles, the remaining chapters the practices.

We have subdivided our software engineering principles into three categories:

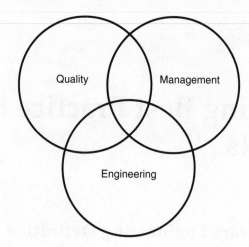

Figure 5.1 Software engineering principles.

- Quality.
- Management.
- Engineering.

5.2 Quality Principles

Quality is not tested into a software product, it is built in by the software process that produces it. One of the elements of this process is effective practice, based on the following quality principles:

- Prevent defects from being introduced.
- Ensure that defects are detected and corrected as early as possible.
- Establish and eliminate the causes as well as the symptoms of defects.
- Independently audit the work for compliance with standards and procedures.

5.2.1 Put Effort into Prevention

One way to avoid defects in a software product is to prevent them from occurring. Consequently, at least as much emphasis should be placed on defect prevention as on detection. There are many different aspects to defect prevention, but it is mainly achieved by the following:

- Appropriate software engineering standards and procedures.

- Independent quality auditing to ensure those standards and procedures are followed.
- Clearly defined staff roles, responsibilities and lines of communication.
- A formal method of accumulating and disseminating lessons learned from past experiences and mistakes.
- High-quality inputs, including software tools and subcontracted software.
- Appropriately trained and experienced staff.
- Tools that make it difficult or impossible to make common classes of error, for example design tools that check data flows, or compilers that check for uninitialized variables.

5.2.2 Detect and Correct Early

The number of defects can be substantially reduced by adopting a strategy for defect prevention, but they will not be entirely eliminated. Consequently, a second line of defence must be to detect and correct defects as soon as they are introduced into the development. The reason for this is simple. The longer defects go undetected, the more expensive they become to correct. Research has shown that a design defect can be up to fifteen times more expensive to correct at the testing stage than at the design stage.

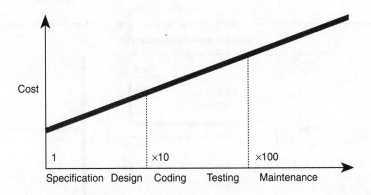

Figure 5.2 Cost of correction by stage found.

It is easy to believe such a statement. For example, if a defect is spotted at the design stage, it can be corrected by modifying the design. If it goes undetected until the testing stage, it will still require the same design modification, but will also demand changes and subsequent regression testing of all code affected by those modifications.

Quality controls, such as reviews, must therefore be applied at all stages of the life cycle, and to all key products of the development including requirements, designs, documentation and code, rather than being left entirely to the testing stage. At that stage, it is too late to correct major mistakes, and more expensive to correct defects.

Several review methods, such as inspections, walkthroughs and technical reviews, are available and are outlined in more detail later.

5.2.3   Eliminate the Cause

Simply detecting and correcting defects is not enough. If the cause of the defect is not also addressed, it is likely that similar defects will occur, either on the same project or on later ones. Detection is concerned with finding and removing the defect. Elimination is concerned with analyzing the cause of the defect. The motivation for this is not to apportion blame, which is counterproductive, but to discover if it was caused by an inadequacy in the process. If it was, the process is modified to prevent it recurring.

Detection involves corrective action at a software project level, for example correcting a design defect resulting from a lack of communication between team members. Elimination involves corrective action at a software process level, for example correcting a defect in the communication procedures between team members.

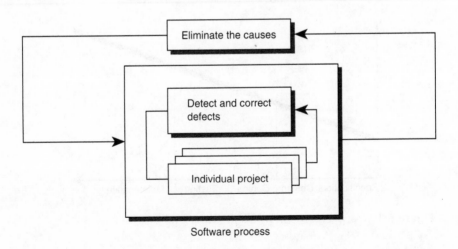

Figure 5.3 Defect elimination.

5.2.4   Audit the Work

The concept of auditing is central to quality and is applied at two levels: process and project.

Process Level

Every organization has a process for developing and maintaining software. The process may not be formally defined or understood and may even be chaotic, but it is still a process. A process level audit assesses the strengths and weaknesses of an organization's current software process in order to address the weaknesses. In this way, the organization can define and maintain a standard software process. This is then used as a yardstick for analyzing and improving the performance of software projects.

A standard process consists of documented standards and procedures that define an environment for developing software, enable discussion of project issues in a common vocabulary, and allow staff to collect and apply experience consistently.

Several methods of conducting such process assessments are presently available. For example, the Software Engineering Institute (SEI) at Carnegie Mellon University have developed a software process assessment methodology that associates a software process with one of five maturity levels.

Project Level

Quality is not imposed on a project, but is controlled and managed from within by the project staff. All staff members bear responsibility for the quality of their own work, and the project manager bears overall responsibility for project quality. However, it is a fundamental principle of quality that the management of quality within a project is validated by staff who are independent of the work that they audit, since nobody can be expected to audit their own work objectively. The purpose of this is twofold: to determine if activities are being carried out in accordance with the standards and procedures laid down by the quality process, and whether those standards and procedures are adequate to ensure the quality of the project in general.

5.3   Management Principles

The development of a software product involves much more than the transformation of a set of stated requirements into software. It always takes place in some business context, which imposes time, resource and budget constraints on the work. This means that project activities must be appropriately planned, scheduled and monitored to take account of these constraints. There is also the issue of communication, both between the developer and the customer, and between members of the development team.

Effective management of these issues is based on the following principles:

- Clearly define the structure, roles, responsibilities and lines of communication between groups and individuals.
- Carefully plan all activities needed to complete the overall task within time, budget, resource and quality constraints.
- Continually monitor progress against plans, and revise plans appropriately when tolerances have been exceeded.
- Refine the detail of plans as knowledge of the task increases.

5.3.1 Define Roles and Responsibilities

Communication is a key element of any project. The larger the number of people involved in a project, the more consciously it needs to be managed. For example, consider the difference between a ten-person-year project performed as one person working on it for ten years, and ten people working on it for one year. For any project to run effectively and efficiently, members of the development team must have an understanding of:

- their roles in the team;
- their responsibilities;
- their areas of authority;
- the lines of communication within the team and with other groups.

5.3.2 Plan the Work

Planning is essential. In any software project, it is important to develop realistic plans for all the activities and risks involved. These plans should describe what activities need to be performed, how they are to be carried out, and with what resources.

Planning has three aspects:

- Technical.
- Quality.
- Resource.

Technical Planning

Technical planning describes what must done in order to build the software (that is to define, design and implement it). An integral part of technical planning is deciding the phases into which the work will be divided, the activities and deliverables associated with each phase, and the milestones along the way.

Quality Planning

While technical planning describes the steps necessary to build the software, quality planning describes the measures needed to ensure that it is built correctly (that is it satisfies all requirements).

This involves defining the standards and procedures which will apply to project activities, and the quality controls applied to the end products of each phase. These will be used at different stages to verify that the products of that stage conform to requirements, and are subject to change control.

Resource Planning

It is not enough just to build the software correctly; it must be built on time and within budget. Every software development project has some time and resource constraints imposed on it, so resource planning to cater for these constraints is essential. This involves estimating the work, allocating resources to it, and scheduling it.

5.3.3   Track Progress against Plans

Plans are useless if the work is not tracked and documented against them, with corrective action being taken when necessary. Small deviations are normal and may require only minor changes to plans or activities. Significant deviations may need more extensive action such as a complete replanning of part (or all) of the original plans.

5.3.4   Progressively Refine the Plans

Planning is an attempt to forecast the future, and is always based on incomplete information. It is thus difficult to be entirely accurate, and the further into the future the planning extends, the more difficult it becomes. The difficulty lies partly in the fact that it is impossible to foresee every eventuality, and partly in the fact that the perception of the task being planned is altered and refined as that task is performed.

There is therefore a need for a two-tier approach to planning. At any given point, there should be plans at two levels: an outline plan, covering long term objectives, activities and priorities at a high level; and a detailed plan, which is a refinement of the outline plan, spanning the immediate future at a greater level of detail.

5.4   Engineering Principles

Despite the use of the term 'software engineering' to describe the process of developing software, many factors distinguish software from other engineering fields. For example, it is relatively recent and more complex than many other engineering processes, with no foundation in physical principles. Nevertheless, a systematic and disciplined approach to software development can be achieved by applying the following principles:

• Determine the requirements and define a solution.
• Break up the solution into clearly defined components.
• Rigorously control the relationships between components.

5.4.1   Analyze the Problem

Before developing a solution, it is important to develop a clear understanding of the problem or need. In software, there are two difficulties in doing this. First, the need is usually expressed in terms of some business or other 'real world' domain. This must be translated into terms that are meaningful in a software context. Second, customers often do not fully understand their own needs, or are not able to articulate them.

5.4.2   Break up the Solution

In all but the most trivial cases, developing a software solution to a customer need is a complex task that is best handled by repeatedly breaking it into a number of less complex tasks. The approach used to develop a solution determines how to break up the solution, while the life cycle model used determines when. For example, an object oriented approach breaks up the solution into objects, while other approaches break it up according to function or data. Similarly, a waterfall life cycle breaks up the entire solution once, before coding commences, while an evolutionary model alternates between design and coding.

5.4.3   Control the Relationships

If a complex system is divided into less complex units, a solution can be implemented more easily. However, all the units must reintegrate into a system that fully satisfies the original requirements. This can only be achieved if the relationships between components are clearly defined and rigorously controlled throughout the development. In a software context, this means controlling the interfaces between the components (be they objects or modules) to ensure that they continue to relate to one another in a consistent and predictable manner.

5.5   Software Engineering Practices

Good software engineering practices provide the means of applying the above software engineering principles to projects. The practices are embedded in appropriate project standards and procedures within an organization. Later chapters describe such practices in some detail. The remainder of this chapter describes the purpose, structure and application of the framework into which these practices have been structured. Conscious effort has been made to make the guidelines as clear as possible without making them dependent on any specific software tools or methodologies.

5.5.1 Purpose of Framework

The main purpose of the framework is to present software developers with a set of software engineering guidelines which:

- are based on current best software engineering practices, as defined in international software engineering standards;
- are compatible with the ISO 9001 international quality standard, the ISO 9000–3 guidelines for software, and the ISO 9004–2 guidelines for services;
- can be applied by different sizes and types of software organizations;
- are focused on individual projects, but contribute to a more general software quality system.

5.5.2 Structure of Framework

The framework breaks down the activities and deliverables of a software development project into three categories:

Life cycle activities. These are concerned with transforming the requirements into a software product, for example analysis, design, and coding, and are described in Chapter 6.

Supporting activities. These are concerned with the technical and organizational management of the life cycle activities, which ensure that the product is built within budget, according to schedule and with the required degree of quality. They are described in Chapter 7.

Organization level activities. These are concerned with improving the organization's standard software process. This involves monitoring its application and measuring its performance at an individual project level. The standard process can then be improved and refined based on the accumulated experience of many projects, and can act as a 'reservoir' of experiences and lessons from which future projects can draw. These activities are described in Chapter 8.

5.5.3 Applying the Framework

Applying the framework in the context of an individual software development organization calls for a flexible rather than a rigid approach. Software projects can vary widely in complexity, size and purpose, and the guidelines must be tailored and interpreted accordingly.

The guidelines can be used as a checklist to evaluate the coverage given by existing organizational standards and practices, or they can be used as a basis for developing or enhancing such organizational procedures, where deficiencies have been revealed.

In either case, the interpretation of certain terms provides the key to resolving any potential difficulties in relating the guidelines to current practice within different organizations. The first thing to note is that specific practices are presented with one of three degrees of emphasis:

Essential practices: these should always be followed.

Important practices: these are strongly recommended and should not be overlooked without strong justification.

Useful practices: these are recommended, but optional.

Another important point to bear in mind is that roles and products described or referenced are essentially 'logical' roles and products. In other words, what constitutes a role or function in the guidelines is not an activity or task performed exclusively by one person. In practice, a single role may be fulfilled by several people, or, alternatively, several roles may be fulfilled by a single individual. Similarly, a product or document in the guidelines need not constitute a separate physical document in practice. In some cases, it may be split across several physical documents, while in others, several documents may be combined into a single physical document.

5.5.4 Relating the Framework to ISO 9001

The structure of the framework and the emphasis of the recommendations are based on good software engineering practice, rather than on the structure or emphasis of ISO 9001 or the 9000–3 guidelines for software. The recommendations are also more detailed than ISO 9001 or ISO 9000–3, but, at a higher level, are consistent with them. This can be seen from Appendix E, which contains a summary of the essential practices, and Appendix D, which cross-references them to ISO 9000–3.

6
Life Cycle Activities

6.1 Overview

Life cycle activities are concerned with transforming a user need into a software product that satisfies the need. The life cycle of a software product starts when the product is conceived, and finishes when it is no longer available for use. It therefore encompasses the operations and maintenance of the software as well as the development. To facilitate managing the life cycle, among other reasons, it is useful to break it up into phases. Each phase has a set of defined inputs, activities and outputs. These phases then form the basis for constructing a life cycle model, which determines how many times the different phases will be executed.

Phase	Purpose	Deliverables
User requirements	Problem definition	User requirements specification
Software requirements	Problem analysis	Software and support service requirements
Architectural design	High level solution	High level software design and support service design
Production	Implementation	Detailed software design Tested software and established support service
Transfer	Handover and installation	Installed software
Maintenance	Software operations and support	Maintained and supported software

Figure 6.1 Life cycle phases

80

This chapter presents a life cycle consisting of six modular phases that can be used to construct any of a number of different life cycle models: requirements, software requirements, architectural design, production, transfer, and maintenance.

Each of the products and activities within a phase has an associated set of standards and practices based on current international standards of good software engineering practice. The structuring of activities into these phases is not arbitrary, but is not 'cast in stone' either. What is most important is the activities themselves and the links between them.

6.2   Life Cycle Approaches

This chapter presents a life cycle consisting of six phases that must occur in any software development project. Many different life cycle models can be derived from these phases, because they have been defined in a reusable and modular way. Some of these models are outlined below.

Waterfall Model

This was the first successful life cycle model to be used, and has been through many different variations since it was first introduced. It advocates a stepwise, 'single shot' approach to software development, and consists of a number of separate phases with feedback loops between adjacent phases.

Some of the problems with this model lie in the difficulty in making changes downstream, and the length of time between the requirements definition and the emergence of software. The latter point can be particularly acute on large and complex projects.

Incremental Model

The incremental model overcomes some of the difficulties of the waterfall model by delivering the software in stages. It follows the waterfall approach to the completion of the architectural design phase, which it then implements and delivers in pieces rather than in one pass.

This approach can provide early feedback to the developer and helps to shorten the time between requirements and implementation. However, incremental delivery demands more organization as well as careful selection of the order in which the parts are delivered, which can place added constraints on the design. In some cases, it may not be possible to deliver parts that are useful without the rest of the system. In addition, if increments are too small, repeated testing can increase overall project costs.

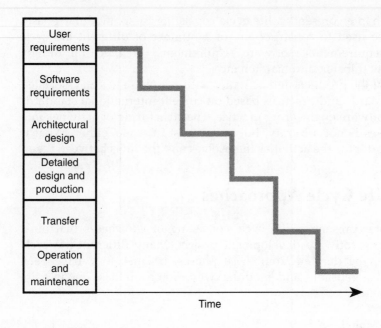

Figure 6.2(a) Life cycle approaches: waterfall model.

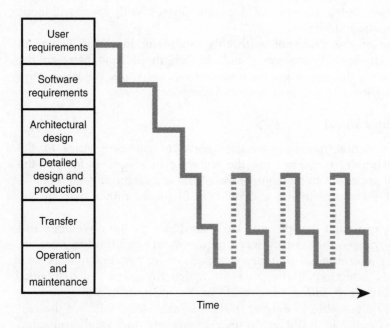

Figure 6.2(b) Life cycle approaches: incremental model.

Evolutionary Model

The evolutionary model differs from the incremental model in that all phases, including requirements and design phases, are repeated (Figure 6.2c). This is particularly useful when initial requirements are poorly understood or unstable. It can also give users an early operational capability. Planning is very important when using the evolutionary model to ensure that the evolutions converge on a desired solution, that each evolution can accommodate any required future evolutionary paths, and that any long-range architectural or usage considerations are addressed to avoid evolving a lot of code that is difficult to change.

The spiral model (IEEE May 1988, Barry Boehm) explicitly incorporates this type of planning, as well as risk analysis and management (Figure 6.2d). Each cycle of the spiral begins with the identification of the objectives of the portion of the product being elaborated, the alternative means of implementation, and the constraints imposed on the alternatives. The alternatives are then evaluated relative to the objectives. Project risks and uncertainties are then identified and evaluated to determine which subsequent steps of the model are executed.

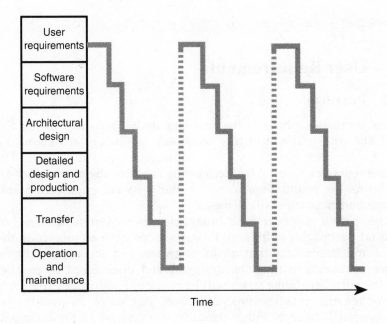

Figure 6.2(c) Life cycle approaches: evolutionary model.

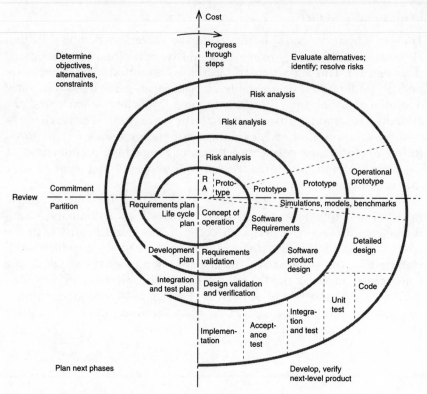

Figure 6.2(d) Life cycle approaches: spiral model (Boehm 1988).

6.3 User Requirements

6.3.1 Purpose

The requirements phase is the problem definition stage in the life cycle. The principal aim of this phase is to refine an idea about the task to be performed by the software, into some form of requirements definition. This defines the scope of the software effort and forms the foundation on which the software engineering and management activities will be based.

The user's support and maintenance requirements are an **essential** part of this definition. First, they can have an impact on the design and implementation of the software, and second, a suitable service environment must be designed and engineered in parallel with the software. Some users will have enough software experience to produce the requirements definition, but more frequently the developer will have to either produce it, or assist in producing it. However, it is **essential** for the user to retain full control over the definition of the user requirements.

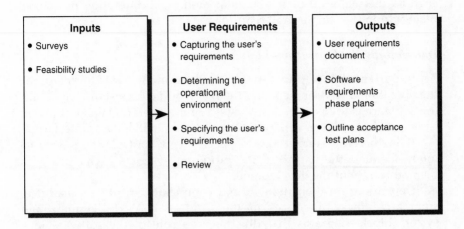

Inputs	User Requirements	Outputs
• Surveys	• Capturing the user's requirements	• User requirements document
• Feasibility studies	• Determining the operational environment	• Software requirements phase plans
	• Specifying the user's requirements	• Outline acceptance test plans
	• Review	

Figure 6.3 Overview of user requirements phase.

6.3.2 Inputs

There are no formal inputs to this phase, but the results of relevant surveys, feasibility studies and so on may prove useful.

6.3.3 Activities

Capturing the User's Requirements

The capture and documentation of the user's requirements is the main activity of this phase. In most software projects either new requirements or changes to existing requirements will occur during the software development stages. But it is still **essential** to try to develop as complete and stable a requirements definition as possible, even for life cycle models that make several passes through the requirements phase. This is what determines the scope of the software effort and is the foundation on which that effort is based.

It is therefore **important** to get the widest possible agreement about requirements from all interested parties through interviews and surveys. It may be **useful** to clarify requirements through user criticism of existing software, or through the development of prototypes to model screen layouts and menu structures.

Whichever way it is approached, requirements definition is an iterative process and several repetitions of the capture activities will probably be needed before a stable and comprehensive requirements definition can be achieved. In the case of an evolutionary life cycle model, this iteration is characterized in the life cycle itself; for others, such as the waterfall or incremental models, the iteration must take place within the 'single shot' requirements phase.

Determining the Operational Environment

An **important** first step in defining user requirements is to determine the operational environment and the real world circumstances in which the software is to operate. A key aspect of the operational environment is the external systems with which the software will have to interface.

It is therefore **important** to specify and control these external interfaces, and the nature of the proposed system's exchanges with them, throughout the development.

Depending on their number and complexity, it may be **useful** to summarize these interfaces in the form of context diagrams and system block diagrams that illustrate the role of the software in a larger system. In cases where the nature of exchanges with external systems is likely to change during development, it is also **useful** to record the information in a separate document.

Specifying the User's Requirements

Once the operational environment has been determined, specific user requirements can then be extracted and organized. These require-ments can be placed into one of three categories:

- Capability.
- Constraint.
- Support.

Capability requirements describe operations and functions actually needed by the user. Constraint requirements place restrictions on the way the software can be built and operated (by specifying that the software use certain protocols, standards, hardware, operating systems and so on). Support requirements describe, for example, requirements for training, level of support and type of support required after delivery.

For capability requirements, it is **useful** to attach performance and accuracy attributes to the requirement, as this can help both in the validation and acceptance testing of the system. For constraint requirements relating to adaptability, portability and security, or for support requirements relating to responsiveness, it is **useful** for the requirement to convey the relative criticality of these functions to the overall system.

The following **important** attributes also need consideration for all categories of requirements:

Identifier. The identifier of a requirement allows you to trace and reference it throughout the development and is unique for each requirement.

Need. Some requirements may be more important to the user than others. The need of a requirement indicates its relative importance to the user, and in particular, identifies essential or non-negotiable requirements.

Stability. During the life cycle of the software some requirements are more likely to change than others. The stability of a requirement measures the likelihood that it will remain unchanged throughout the life cycle.

Source. The source of a requirement identifies the user, user group, external document or whatever other source supplied the requirement.

Clarity. The clarity of a requirement is a measure of its unambiguity. Since a requirement should have only one interpretation, terms with multiple interpretations need to be qualified or replaced.

Verifiability. The verifiability of a requirement is a measure of the extent to which it is possible to check its incorporation into the design and test its implementation in the software.

Priority. For incremental delivery of the software, the priority of each requirement to the user should be stated, so that the developer can decide the production schedule.

Review

It is **essential** to review all phase outputs at the end of the phase, and to record the results of these reviews. It is **essential** in the review of the user's requirements to involve representatives of the users, operators, developers and managers concerned with the development and operation of the proposed software system.

Depending on the business relationship between the user and the developer, a formal contract may be signed at this stage, if this has not already been done. In drawing up a contract, the following **important** aspects of the relationship should be defined and agreed by both parties:

• Developer's responsibility with regard to subcontracted work.
• Terminology used in the contract and in the requirements definition.
• Criteria for acceptance of the completed software by the user.
• Arrangements for handling changes in the user's requirements during development of the software.
• Arrangements for handling problems detected after acceptance, including quality-related claims and complaints.
• Definition of support service levels and other aspects of the support and maintenance of the finished software.

6.3.4 Outputs

The main outputs from the requirements definition phase are the user requirements document, software requirements phase plans, and an updated outline acceptance test plan. In addition, it is **essential** to update the outline project plan with any impacts the phase may have had.

User Requirements Document

It is **essential** to produce a user requirements document that contains a precise and consistent statement of all known user requirements. It is also **essential** to ensure that the document gives a general description of the user's expectation of the software, and that it defines all constraints that the user wishes to place on any solution. It is **essential** to maintain the document under adequate change control procedures, agreed by the user and developer.

Software Requirements Phase Plans

These contain the detailed plans for the project management, configuration management, verification, and quality assurance activities and procedures, for the software requirements phase.

Outline Acceptance Test Plans

These plans describe the approach to demonstrating that the software will satisfy the stated user requirements.

6.4   Software Requirements

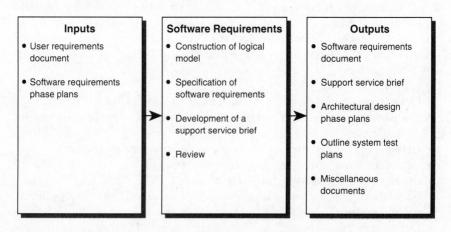

Figure 6.4 Overview of software requirements phase.

6.4.1 Purpose

The user and the developer have different views of a software system. The user views the software from a business or operational viewpoint, while the developer's view is of a more technical nature. The purpose of the software requirements phase is to reconcile these different views by expressing the user requirements in terms that are more meaningful in a software context, which can be more readily developed into a software design.

This is done by analyzing the statement of user requirements and producing a set of software requirements, which are a clear and coherent statement, in software terms, of what the software is expected to do.

6.4.2 Inputs

The inputs to the software requirements phase are:

• User requirements document.
• Software requirements phase plans.

6.4.3 Activities

It is **essential** to carry out the activities of this phase in accordance with the software requirements phase plans, and to monitor and document progress against the plans at regular intervals. Since the software requirements represent the basis on which the software will be designed, it is **important** to base this view on a model of the system that has been constructed using a recognized and docu-mented method.

The major stage in the building of this model is the construction of an implementation-independent, or logical, model of the system from which the software requirements can be extracted and specified.

Construction of Logical Model

It is **essential** for the developer to construct a logical model of the system as the basis for producing the software requirements, and to document it in the software requirements document. In constructing this model, it is **useful** to break the software down into a hierarchy of smaller components. Each level of the hierarchy refines the level of detail of the one above. An **important** part of the development of this hierarchy is the use of walkthroughs, reviews and inspections to ensure that the detail of each level is agreed before proceeding to the next level. Every effort must be made to develop a good model, since it is the basis on which the architectural design is developed. **Important** characteristics of a good model are:

Components. Each component has a single, clearly defined purpose, which can be inferred from its name, and is defined at an appropriate level in the hierarchy. For example, 'Validate Date Field' would not appear at the same level as 'Input Records'.

Interfaces. Interfaces are minimized, allowing components with weak coupling (fewer links) to be more easily derived at the design stage.

Decomposition. At each level, a component should be decomposed into no more than seven sub-components. If this is not possible, examine whether the component belongs at a higher level.

Omission of implementation information. The model omits implementation information, such as reference to files, records, modules and so on.

Attributes. Performance attributes of each component, such as capacity, speed and response time, are stated and critical components are identified.

Specification of Software Requirements

Once the logical model has been constructed, the software requirements can then be extracted and classified. It is **important** to describe software requirements rigorously, and to state them in quantitative terms, as this facilitates their verification. Depending on the application area, the use of specification techniques such as state diagrams, which are more formal than natural language, can be **useful.**

As with user requirements, it is **useful** to classify software requirements into appropriate categories. Although many different classifications of software requirements can be conceived, the following categories should prove sufficient for most purposes:

Functional requirements. These define what the software has to do and are derived directly from the logical model.

Performance requirements. These specify quantitative values for measurable entities such as frequency, speed and capacity. Qualitative statements of these values, such as 'quick response' or 'large capacity', should always be avoided.

Interface requirements. These specify elements with which the system must interact or communicate, and are classified in terms of hardware, software and communications interfaces.

Usability requirements. These specify how the software will interact with human operators and include all user interface and man-machine interaction requirements.

Resource requirements. These specify upper limits on physical resources such as memory, disk space and processing power.

Verification requirements. These specify how the software will be verified, and include simulation and emulation requirements, or requirements for interfacing with a test environment.

Acceptance requirements. These specify constraints on how the software is to be validated by the user.

Documentation requirements. These specify project-specific requirements for documentation, in addition to those described in these guidelines.

Security requirements. These specify requirements for securing the system against threats to confidentiality, integrity and availability.

Portability requirements. These specify the ease of porting to other hardware and software platforms.

Quality requirements. These specify attributes of the software that ensure its fitness for purpose.

Reliability requirements. These specify acceptable average time intervals between failures of various severities.

Maintainability requirements. These specify ease of fault repair and modification to incorporate new requirements.

Safety requirements. These specify requirements necessary to reduce possible damage as a result of software failure.

In addition to classification, the following **important** attributes need to be defined for each software requirement (they are identical to the user requirement attributes, but are repeated for ease of reference):

Identifier. The identifier of a requirement allows you to trace and reference it throughout the development, and is unique for each requirement.

Need. Some requirements may be more **important** to the user than others. The need of a requirement indicates its relative importance, and in particular, identifies essential or non-negotiable requirements.

Stability. During the life cycle of the software, some requirements are more likely to change than others. The stability of a requirement measures the likelihood that it will remain unchanged throughout the life cycle.

Source. Each software requirement should reference the user requirement from which it is derived.

Clarity. The clarity of a requirement is a measure of its unambiguity. Since a requirement should have only one interpretation, terms with multiple interpretations need to be qualified or replaced.

Verifiability. The verifiability of a requirement is a measure of the extent to which it is possible to check its incorporation into the design and test its implementation in the software.

Priority. For incremental delivery of the software, the priority of each requirement should be identified so that the developer can determine the production schedule.

Development of a Support Service Brief

Once the completed software has been delivered, installed and accepted by the user, it will have to be maintained and supported if it is to continue to meet evolving user needs. This support must be provided through a support (and maintenance) service, supplied either by the developer, or a third party maintenance and support organization. It is **essential** to define, design, test and implement this service as rigorously as the software it supports.

The support service brief defines the user's support and maintenance needs as a set of requirements and instructions, based on the support requirements from the previous phase, and the related service organization's capabilities. These form the basis for the design of the support service.

Review

It is **essential** to review all outputs of the software requirements phase formally at the end of the phase, and to record the results. An **important** part of these activities is a technical review of the software requirements, involving appropriate user, operations, development and management representatives. Technical reviews are discussed in Section 7.4.2.

6.4.4 Outputs

The outputs from this phase are the software requirements document, the support service brief, architectural design phase plans, the outline system test plan, and miscellaneous documents. It is also **essential** to update the outline project plan to incorporate any impacts the phase may have had.

Software Requirements Document

It is **essential** to produce and maintain a software requirements document under configuration management. This document must:

- be complete and cover all requirements stated in the user requirements document;
- avoid implementation details and terminology, except where there are user constraints to this effect;
- describe functions in terms of what they must do rather than how they must do it.

It is **useful** to include a table showing how user requirements correspond to software requirements. Any user requirements that are not met, or cannot be satisfied must be resolved with the user. Any necessary changes to the user requirements must be made subject to configuration management.

It is **important** to include the outputs of any analysis methods, such as data flow diagrams, in the document to enhance the understanding of the specific requirements. In some cases it is **useful** to write the document in a natural language, as this will render it more readable to the user. Even if the application area is such that these requirements can be more readily expressed in a formal specification language, it is still **important** to incorporate explanatory natural language text into the document.

Support Service Brief

This defines the user's support needs and the related service organization's capabilities (usually the developer) as a set of requirements and instructions that form the basis for the design of a support service.

Architectural Design Phase Plans

These contain the detailed plans for the project management, configuration management, verification, and quality assurance activities, and procedures for the architectural design phase.

Outline System Test Plans

These outline the approach to demonstrating that the software satisfies all software requirements.

Miscellaneous Documents

Progress reports, audit reports, configuration status accounts and various other documents will also be outputs of this phase. It is **essential** to archive this documentation in an appropriate way.

6.5 Architectural Design

6.5.1 Purpose

This is the 'solution phase' of the life cycle. The main purpose is to establish a framework for developing the software. This is achieved by developing the logical, implementation-independent model of the software requirements phase into a physical, implementation-dependent model.

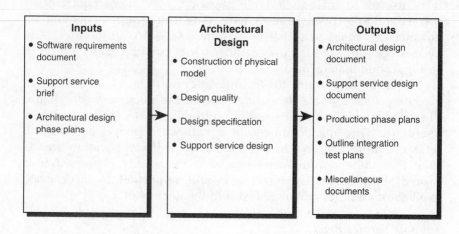

Figure 6.5 Overview of architectural design phase.

6.5.2 Inputs

The inputs to the architectural design phase are:

• Software requirements document.
• Support service brief.
• Architectural design phase plans.

6.5.3 Activities

It is **essential** to carry out the activities of this phase according to the detailed architectural design phase plans, and to monitor and document progress against these plans at regular intervals. It is also **important** to adopt a recognized method of design, and to apply it consistently throughout the phase.

Construction of the Physical Model

It is **essential** to construct a physical model, describing the design of the software in implementation terminology. It is **important** to derive this physical model from the logical model of the software requirements phase and to construct it by breaking the software down into a hierarchy of components according to a partitioning method, such as functional decomposition, or classes of objects. It is also **important** for this hierarchy to consist of distinct levels, and for each component to occupy a well-defined place within a given level. It is therefore **important** that the method used for this decomposition allow a top-down approach.

It is **important** for the architectural design to specify only the upper three or four levels. The lower levels should be left to the detailed design stage of the production phase. There are several advantages to this design approach. First, by demanding that lower levels behave as 'black boxes', with only their functionality and interfaces defined to the higher levels, unnecessary information is suppressed. Second, there is a greater likelihood that the lower level components of the design will be sufficiently independent to allow their detailed design and coding to proceed in parallel.

In addition, it allows different levels of the design to be described at an appropriate level of abstraction. For example, the terms 'file', 'record' and 'byte' would appear at different levels in the design of a file-handling system.

Design Quality

It is **important** to make designs adaptable, efficient and understandable, since this makes them easier to maintain. A design that meets these criteria will normally display simplicity of form and function. It is therefore **useful** to measure some aspects of the design, such as the number of interfaces per component. In addition to these metrics, the following guidelines may also be **useful** in evolving the design:

- Maximize the degree to which the activities within each component are related.
- Minimize the number of distinct items that are passed between components.
- Ensure that a component's position in the hierarchy reflects the function it performs.
- Ensure that no component is decomposed into more than seven sub-components at any given level. If this is not possible, examine whether the component belongs at a higher level.
- Remove duplication between components by creating new component(s) to carry out the common function.

In short, designs should be modular, with minimal coupling between components and maximum cohesion within components.

It is **important** to review each design component against the various non-functional software requirements (for example performance, operational, portability and so on) to ensure that these requirements are engineered into the final software product.

There is no unique design for any software system, so studies and trade-offs between different design options will usually form part of the design process. In some cases, prototyping can provide a **useful** method of evaluating different design approaches and verifying design assumptions.

Although it is **important** to reflect only the selected design in the design documentation, it is **useful** to document and explain any other solutions that were rejected. This can be done in a project history document that can then be consulted by future projects.

Design Specification

The architectural design is effectively the fully documented physical model of the proposed software system, so it is **essential** to document both data and control flows between components, for each level of the design. For each design component, it is **essential** to define the following information:

- Input data.
- Functions to be performed.
- Output data.

Although it can be **useful** to define data inputs and outputs in terms of data structures, it is **essential** to document any data structures that interface components, with at least the following information:

- a description of each element;
- relationships between elements;
- range of possible values for each element;
- initial values of each element.

It is **important**, at this stage, to estimate, in terms of speed, memory and storage, the computer resources that will be required in the development and operational environments, and to document them with the architectural design.

Support Service Design

The design of the support service is developed from the service brief outlined in the previous phase, and has two main components:

Service Specification. This defines the service to be provided.
Delivery Specification. This defines the means and methods by which the service will be delivered.

Since the service and delivery specifications are interdependent and interact throughout the support service design process, it is **essential** to develop them together. It is also **essential** to apply the same quality principles to the design of the support service as are applied to the design of the software.

In developing the service design, it is **important** to:

- plan for variations in the service demand which might affect the service flow;
- anticipate the effect of service failure, including failure of aspects of the service beyond the service supplier's control;
- build contingency plans for such anticipated failures into the service and delivery specifications.

Review

It is **essential** to review all phase outputs at the end of the phase, and to document results. An **important** part of these activities is a technical review (see Section 7.4.2) of the architectural design, to ensure that there are no major open points or uncertainties. Review participants should include appropriate representatives of the users, operators, developers and managers concerned.

6.5.4 Outputs

The outputs from the architectural design phase are the architectural design document, the support service design document, production phase plans, the outline integration test plan, and miscellaneous documents. It is **essential** to update the outline project plans to reflect any impact the phase may have had.

Architectural Design Document

The architectural design document is an **essential** document, which must be maintained under configuration control. It summarizes the solution and is the kernel from which the detailed design, and subsequently the coding, is produced. It is therefore **essential** for this document to:

- define all of the major components of the software and the interfaces between them;
- define or reference all external interfaces between the software and its operational software environment;
- be complete: every software requirement must be traceable to a component of the design;
- be sufficiently detailed to allow a detailed implementation plan, covering the remainder of the development, to be drawn up.

It is **useful** to include a table showing how the software requirements correspond to components of the design. Any software requirements that are not met, or cannot be satisfied must be traced back to their corresponding user requirements and resolved with the user. Any necessary changes to the user or software requirements must be made subject to configuration management.

Support Service Design Document

This **essential** document contains the completed design for the support service outlined during the software requirements phase, and consists of the service specification and the delivery specification. The service specification defines the service to be provided. It is **essential** to ensure that it:

- contains a complete and precise statement of the service to be provided, including those characteristics of the service that are subject to customer evaluation;
- defines a standard of acceptability, either quantitative or comparative, for each service characteristic.

The delivery specification defines the means and methods by which the service defined in the service specification will be delivered. It is **essential** to ensure that it:

- contains procedures describing how the service is to be delivered;
- defines a standard of acceptability, either quantitative or comparative, for each service delivery characteristic;
- identifies resource requirements for service delivery, describing the equipment, facilities and personnel necessary to fulfil the service specification;
- identifies the extent of reliance of the service delivery on third party products or services.

Production Phase Plans

This contains the detailed plans for the project management, configuration management, verification, and quality assurance activities and procedures, for the detailed design and coding phase.

Outline Integration Test Plans

These plans outline the approach to demonstrating that the interfaces between software components conform to the architectural design.

Miscellaneous Documents

Progress reports, audit reports, configuration status accounts and various other documents will also be outputs of this phase. It is **essential** for the project to archive this documentation.

6.6   Production

6.6.1   Purpose

This is the implementation phase of the life cycle: its main purpose is to expand the architectural design into a detailed design, and then to code, document and test it.

6.6.2   Inputs

The inputs to the production phase are the:

- Architectural design document.
- Support service design document.
- Integration test plans.
- System test plans.
- Production phase plans.

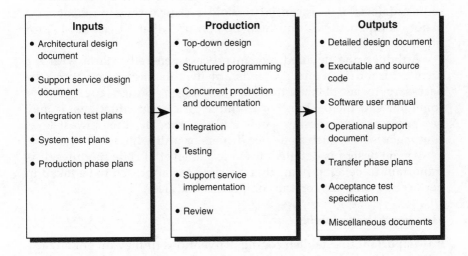

Inputs	Production	Outputs
• Architectural design document	• Top-down design	• Detailed design document
• Support service design document	• Structured programming	• Executable and source code
• Integration test plans	• Concurrent production and documentation	• Software user manual
• System test plans	• Integration	• Operational support document
• Production phase plans	• Testing	• Transfer phase plans
	• Support service implementation	• Acceptance test specification
	• Review	• Miscellaneous documents

Figure 6.6 Overview of production phase.

6.6.3   Activities

It is **essential** to carry out production phase activities according to the detailed production phase plans defined in the previous phase and to monitor and document progress against these plans at regular intervals.

It is **important** to base the detailed design and production of the software on the following principles:

- Top-down design.
- Structured programming.
- Concurrent production and documentation.

Top-down Design

One of the first activities of the production phase is to decompose the lower levels of the architectural design until they can be expressed as modules in the selected programming language. This process is performed using stepwise refinement. It is **important** to keep the steps of refinement small, as it makes review and verification easier.

It is **important** to review and agree the detailed design, layer by layer during its development. It is also **important** to use design walkthroughs (see Section 7.4.2) to ensure the design is understood by all concerned, and to use inspections by qualified personnel to reduce defects. It is **essential** to hold a critical review whenever a major component is finished, to ensure that it is ready for implementation.

Although the detailed design process generally starts with the architectural design and proceeds downwards, it may sometimes be necessary to adopt a 'bottom-up' or 'out-in' design approach for some parts of the design. For example, in certain situations, it may be necessary to design and code some of the lowest-level components first, such as device drivers or utility libraries.

As the design is detailed down to the level of code modules, it is **important** to develop plans that describe the approach to be taken in performing unit tests on the completed modules.

Structured Programming

It is **important** to establish coding conventions (if they do not already exist at an organizational level) and to document or reference them with the detailed design. These cover the following aspects of coding:

- presentation, principally header information and comment layout;
- naming conventions for programs, subprograms, files, variables and data;
- module size limitations;
- the use of library routines such as operating system, commercial library and project-specific utility library routines;
- definition of constants;

- the use of compiler-specific features not in the language standard;
- error handling.

It is also **important** to ensure that code is well structured and that it follows these guidelines:

- each module has a single entry and exit point;
- control flow proceeds, as much as possible, from the beginning to the end of the module;
- related code is blocked together, rather than being dispersed around the module;
- branching out of a module is only performed under prescribed conditions;
- supplementary code, such as code included to assist the test process, is readily identifiable and easy to disable and remove.

After modules have been coded and compiled, it is **important** to subject them to walkthroughs or inspections, to verify that their implementation conforms to their design.

Concurrent Production and Documentation

It is **important** to ensure that documentation of the design assumptions, function, and interface of the software proceeds at the same time as the coding. When a module has been documented, coded and compiled, unit testing can begin.

Integration

It is **important** to ensure that integration of the process of building a software system by combining components into a working entity proceeds in an orderly function-by-function sequence. This allows the software's operational capabilities to be demonstrated early, increasing management confidence that the project is progressing satisfactorily.

It is **essential** to control the integration process using the software configuration management procedures defined for the production phase. One top-down approach to integration is to use 'stubs' to represent lower-level modules, and to replace them as the modules are completed and tested. On the other hand, the need for shared components to be made available early may initially require a bottom-up approach.

Testing

Testing is the process of exercising software to confirm that it satisfies specified requirements and identify differences between expected and actual results. Before testing activities begin, it is **essential** to have developed and documented detailed test designs, cases and procedures for each of the following types of testing activities:

- Unit.
- Integration.
- System.
- Acceptance.

Unit Testing. 'Black box' testing checks that for a given set of inputs, the module produces the correct set of outputs, but it does not check the method used to produce the results. 'White box' testing, on the other hand, checks that the correct paths through the code are executed under given circumstances. It is **important** to carry out both black box and white box testing on each module, to establish whether the module is performing as it should. It is **important** to ensure that the white box testing verifies that every statement in the module is successfully executed at least once, and that the most probable paths through a module are identified and tested.

Integration Testing. It is **essential** to direct integration tests at verifying that all of the system's major components, as identified in the architectural design, interface correctly. This involves ensuring that all data exchanged across an interface agree with the data structure specifications in the architectural design, and the control flows identified in that design have been implemented.

System Testing. After successful unit and integration testing, the process of testing the integrated software can start. This testing can be performed in either the development or the target environment. The **essential** goal of system testing is to verify that the system complies with the system objectives stated in the software requirements document.

Acceptance Testing. Acceptance tests validate the software in its operational environment, and are carried out during the early stages of the transfer phase. It is **important** to base the acceptance tests on the user requirements as stated in the user requirements document, and to involve users in these tests.

Support Service Implementation

It is **important** to implement the support service defined in the Support Service Design Document in parallel with the implementation of the software. This will ensure that the service is in place in time for the transfer phase. In some cases, implementation of the support service may simply consist of assigning a telephone line where queries can be received and followed up. In other cases, it may be a project in its own right, involving the establishment of localization and distribution facilities with extensive technical support and training.

It is **essential** to define responsibility and authority clearly for all support service activities. It is also **essential** to ensure that service staff have the technical knowledge and communications skills needed to perform their duties effectively. Communications skills are particularly important for staff who deal directly with the user. If there are deficiencies in these areas, it is **important** to organize appropriate training to rectify the situation.

In addition, it is **essential** to acquire the material resources identified in the support service design and to have them in place for the start of the service. These resources include service provisioning equipment and operational and technical documentation.

Review

It is **essential** to review all phase outputs formally, and to record the results. An **important** part of the review is a technical review (see Section 7.4.2) of the reports from the verification and testing activities, to decide whether the software is ready for transfer. It is **important** to ensure that the users, project managers, and engineers are appropriately represented at the review.

6.6.4   Outputs

The outputs from the production phase are the detailed design document, executable and source code, software user manual, operational support document, transfer phase plans, acceptance test specification, and miscellaneous documents. It is **essential** to update the outline project plans to reflect any impacts the phase has had.

Detailed Design Document

The detailed design document evolves as the design proceeds to the lowest levels of decomposition, and is an **essential** document. It is therefore **important** to write it in parallel with detailed design, coding and testing. It is **essential** to ensure that it:

• defines, or references, design and coding standards and tools;
• is complete and accounts for all software requirements.

It is **useful** to include a table showing how the software requirements correspond to components of the detailed design. It is

essential to trace any software requirements that are not met, or cannot be satisfied back to their corresponding user requirements, and to resolve these with the user. Any necessary changes to requirements, designs or code must be made under the appropriate configuration management procedures.

Executable and Source Code

It is **essential** to include in this output all items necessary to execute and modify any part of the software produced by the project, as well as a configuration item list identifying all deliverable code.

Software User Manual

The software user manual is developed concurrently with coding and testing, so it is **important** to start its development early. It is also **important** to establish the document's readership, as this affects the way the document is structured and written (for example whether the style should be tutorial or reference).

Operational Support Document

This document describes the implementation of the operational support service that has been developed from the support service design document.

Transfer Phase Plans

These contain the detailed plans for project management, configuration management, verification, and quality assurance activities and procedures for the transfer phase.

Acceptance Test Specification

This describes the designs, cases and procedures for the acceptance testing activities that will be conducted during the transfer phase, after the software has been installed in its operational environment.

Miscellaneous Documents

Test reports, progress reports, audit reports, configuration status accounts and various other documents will also be outputs of this phase. It is **essential** for the project to archive this documentation.

6.7   Transfer

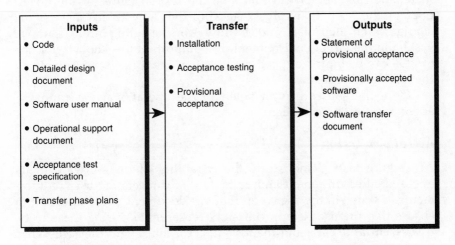

Inputs	Transfer	Outputs
• Code	• Installation	• Statement of provisional acceptance
• Detailed design document	• Acceptance testing	
	• Provisional acceptance	• Provisionally accepted software
• Software user manual		
• Operational support document		• Software transfer document
• Acceptance test specification		
• Transfer phase plans		

Figure 6.7 Overview of transfer phase.

6.7.1   Purpose

This is the handover phase of the life cycle. Its purpose is to install the software in the operational environment and have it provisionally accepted by the user by demonstrating that it fulfils all of the requirements described in the user requirements document.

6.7.2   Inputs

The inputs to the transfer phase are the:

- Code.
- Detailed design document.
- Software user manual.
- Operational support document.
- Acceptance test specification.
- Transfer phase plans.

6.7.3   Activities

It is **essential** to carry out transfer phase activities in accordance with the transfer phase plans laid down in the previous phase, and to monitor and document progress against the plans at regular intervals.

Installation

Installation of the software may be the responsibility of the developer or the user. It involves checking the deliverables against the configuration item list and building or installing an executable system in the target environment. It is **important** to establish that the system can be built from components that are directly modifiable by the maintenance team.

Once the software is installed in the operational environment, acceptance testing can begin.

Acceptance Testing

Acceptance tests demonstrate the capability of the software in its operational environment and validate that it meets the user requirements as stated in the user requirements document. It is **important** to ensure that the user is appropriately represented during these tests. It is **essential** to carry out the tests in accordance with the acceptance test plans, designs, cases and procedures outlined in the acceptance test plans and specification. It is also **essential** to record and document the results of these tests.

Provisional Acceptance

Once the acceptance testing activities have been completed, a review of the acceptance test reports is held by appropriate representatives of the user and the developer, to determine whether or not the software will be provisionally accepted. If it is found that the software is ready for operational use, a statement of provisional acceptance is issued by appropriate user representatives and sent to the developer. It is **important** to identify in the acceptance test plans the acceptance tests necessary for the provisional acceptance of the software.

6.7.4   Outputs

The outputs from this phase are as follows:

Statement of provisional acceptance. This indicates the provisional acceptance of the software by the user and marks the end of the transfer phase.

Provisionally accepted software. This consists of all the outputs of the previous phase and all modifications found necessary during the transfer phase.

Software transfer document. This document identifies the software that is being transferred, in the form of a configuration item list, and describes software build and installation procedures. It also contains a summary of acceptance test reports and all documentation about software changes performed during the transfer phase.

6.8   Maintenance

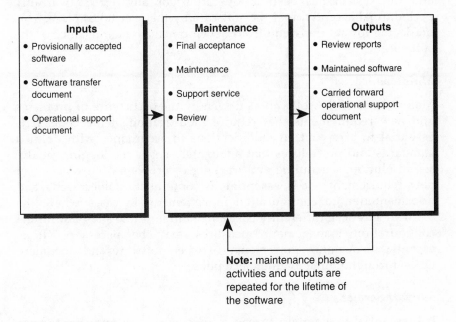

Inputs	Maintenance	Outputs
• Provisionally accepted software	• Final acceptance	• Review reports
	• Maintenance	• Maintained software
• Software transfer document	• Support service	• Carried forward operational support document
• Operational support document	• Review	

Note: maintenance phase activities and outputs are repeated for the lifetime of the software

Figure 6.8 Overview of maintenance phase.

6.8.1 Purpose

The purpose of the maintenance phase is to ensure that the software continues to satisfy the user's needs. This involves fixing previously undetected defects as well as making enhancements to satisfy new or changing requirements. It also involves providing the necessary level of continued support service to satisfy technical support, training needs and so on.

6.8.2 Inputs

The inputs to the maintenance phase are:

• Provisionally accepted software.
• Software transfer document.
• Operational support document.

6.8.3   Activities

Final Acceptance

Some user requirements need a period of operation of the software to verify completely. After all requirements have been fully verified and the system has been in operation for any agreed warranty period, final acceptance of the software by the user takes place. This marks the formal transition from development to maintenance of the software.

Maintenance

Maintenance of the software is driven by the occurrence of problems and new requirements that require modification of the code. It is **essential** to carry out all modifications in accordance with defined standards and procedures that adequately cover the logging, analysis, resolution, scheduling and tracking of problem occurrences and new requirements. It is **essential** to continue to subject code and documentation to configuration management. In cases where the software has been differently customized in multiple sites, additional configuration management measures may be necessary. It is **essential** to maintain consistency between software and documentation throughout the maintenance phase.

Support Service

It is **essential** to maintain agreed service levels. An **important** factor in this is the recording and monitoring of the levels and nature of service requests, the number of outstanding requests, the average resolution time per request, and so on, to obtain adequate warning of impending problems.

Review

It is **essential** to review and evaluate periodically all maintenance phase standards and procedures to determine their effectiveness. It is also **essential** to regularly review both the specification and the delivery of the support service, to ensure that they continue to meet the user needs.

7

Supporting Activities

7.1 Overview

There is a great deal more to the life cycle of a software product than development and maintenance activities. The activities and products of each phase must be closely managed, reviewed and controlled if the project is to be successful. This chapter describes the activities and practices, both technical and organizational, necessary for the effective management of the life cycle. The activities have been arranged into four main categories: Project Management, Configuration Management, Verification, and Quality Assurance.

Unlike the earlier life cycle activities, which are performed at different stages of the life cycle, all of the above activities must be carried out in every phase, if the project is to succeed in delivering the software on time, within budget and to the required quality. An **essential** part of this application is the development of plans to cover these activities.

There are two **important** levels to this planning: the outline and the detailed. Outline plans are prepared at the commencement of the project and, at any given project phase, cover the remainder of the project at an outline level of detail. Outline plans are complemented by detailed plans covering the next project phase at a high level of detail. Before the end of each stage of the project, it is therefore **essential** to:

- Update the outline project plans to reflect any impact that the stage may have on overall dependencies, objectives, priorities and so on.
- Produce detailed plans covering the supporting activities for the next stage of the project.

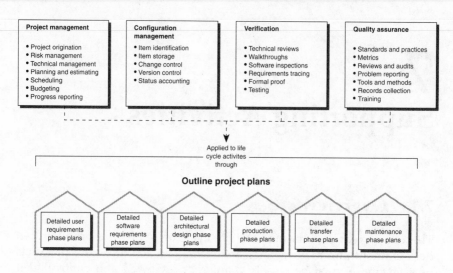

Figure 7.1 Supporting activities.

7.2   Project Management

7.2.1   Purpose

Project management is defined in the IEEE standard as 'the process of planning, organizing, staffing, monitoring, controlling and leading a software project'. Project management therefore must define the management and technical functions and activities of the project. These functions and activities must be planned and documented, and the plans must be reviewed, refined and updated as the project progresses.

7.2.2   Activities

Organizing the Project

Organization of project activities is a key function of project management. It is **essential** to define the development phases of the project, together with the required entry and exit criteria for each phase, and the inputs and outputs of each phase. In addition to defining the tasks, it is **essential** for project management to define the team structure for the project. That is, positions in the project team should be sufficiently defined so that each member has clear responsibilities and lines of authority.

It is also a project management function to decide objectives and priorities at each stage of the project. It is **essential** to document any assumptions, dependencies and constraints that have influenced these decisions.

Risk Analysis

Risk management is about identifying and controlling the factors critical to the success of a project, with a view to reducing the risk levels faced by the project. It is therefore **essential** for project management to:

* identify and assess the risks to a project;
* prioritize the risks, and devise plans to reduce them;
* monitor the plans and re-evaluate the risks throughout the project.

The type of risks that a project may face include:

* clarity and stability of user requirements;
* availability of adequate resources;
* staff training and experience;
* technical novelty of the project;
* short timescales.

Technical Management

Project management is responsible for selecting the project methods and tools that will be used throughout the life cycle, and for organizing the configuration management and verification activities. In doing so, it is **essential** for them to work within the constraints of organization-wide standards and procedures.

Estimation and Scheduling

A key project management activity is the estimation of project resources and time. The determination of these estimates can be enhanced by breaking the project down into small tasks, which are more easily estimated.

One of the most fundamental tools for planning and control of project activities is the Work Breakdown Structure, which describes the hierarchy of tasks and work packages to be carried out on a project. An **essential** part of project management plans for each phase is a Work Breakdown Structure that:

* covers all software development activities for the phase, including verification activities;
* specifies start and end dates for each work package;
* contains detailed product-orientated work packages of short

enough duration to permit a high level of progress visibility;
- defines work package tasks in sufficient detail to permit individuals and small groups to work independently of the rest of the project;
- relates work package completion dates to key project milestones.

Project Tracking

It is **essential** to monitor project progress continually, and to track it against plans. Regular progress review meetings and progress reports are an **important** part of the tracking process. They provide visibility of development activity at regular intervals, and can be used to report progress to people outside the immediate project team.

7.2.3   Coverage of Project Management Plans

Project management plans deal with the organization, management, budgeting and scheduling of the project. It is **essential** to document these plans, giving adequate cover to the following areas:

Introduction

- Overview.
- Deliverables.
- Reference materials.
- Definition of terms.

Project Organization

- Life cycle model.
- Organizational structure.
- Organizational boundaries and interfaces.
- Responsibilities.

Managerial Process

- Management objectives and priorities.
- Assumptions, dependencies and constraints.
- Risk management.
- Monitoring and controlling mechanisms.
- Staffing.

Technical Process

- Methods, tools and techniques.
- Software documentation.
- Support functions.

Work Packages, Schedule and Budget

- Work packages.
- Dependencies.
- Resource requirements.
- Budget and resource allocation.
- Schedule.

7.2.4   Evolution of Project Management Plans

It is **essential** to plan, document and monitor all project management activities appropriately. Like all planning activities, long-term project management plans are produced at the start of the project and these evolve into more detailed plans as the project progresses. The evolution of project management plans is outlined below.

User Requirements. User requirements project management plans define in detail the project management activities for the user requirements phase.

Software Requirements. Revised project estimates, based on the number, level and stability of user requirements, are incorporated into the outline project plan. Project management activities for the phase are covered in detail by the software requirements project management plans.

Architectural Design. Refined project estimates, based on the number, level, stability and quality of the software requirements and any other estimation criteria normally utilized, are incorporated into the outline plan, in addition to any other refinements. Architectural design project management plans cover in detail all project management activities for the phase.

Production. An **important** element of project management plans for the production phase is a detailed Work Breakdown Structure derived from the decomposition of the software into components. It is **important** to ensure that this structure illustrates the relationships between coding, integration and testing activities. Refined project estimates, based on the structure, are incorporated into the outline plan. The work breakdown structure and schedule in the production phase plans is refined in parallel with the detailed design and coding of the software. In order to maintain a high level of project visibility throughout the production phase (that is the degree to which progress is measurable), no single work package in the refined work breakdown structure should exceed one person-month.

Transfer. Installation work packages and schedules are documented in the project management plans for the transfer phase.

Maintenance. Staffing, responsibilities and authorities defined in the project management plans for the maintenance phase should not conflict with those of the support service. Maintenance phase plans need to be revised and updated at regular intervals throughout the maintenance phase in order to remain relevant and effective.

7.3   Configuration Management

7.3.1   Purpose

It is **essential** to subject major software items, including documentation, design, code, files and data, to appropriate configuration management procedures. This is both a technical and a managerial activity, and is defined by the IEEE standard as the process of:

* identifying and defining the configuration items in a system;
* controlling the release and change of configuration items;
* recording and reporting the status of configuration items;
* verifying the completeness and correctness of configuration items.

It is **essential** for configuration management procedures to establish a means of identifying, storing and changing software items throughout the life cycle.

7.3.2   Activities

Configuration Identification

A configuration item can be described as a collection of software elements, treated as a unit, for the purpose of configuration management.

Unambiguous identification of software elements is the key to effective software configuration management. It is therefore **essential** for every configuration item to have an identifier which distinguishes it from other items with different requirements and implementation. It is **essential** for the identifier to include a version number which identifies the stage of evolution of the configuration item, which is updated as the configuration item changes. If the configuration item is a document, it is **important** for the identifier to contain an issue number, marking the major changes, and a revision number, marking the minor ones.

An **essential** property of the configuration identification system is that it must be capable of accommodating new configuration items without requiring changes to the identifiers of existing ones.

It is **essential** for each code module to contain a header which, along with any component information, contains the following details:

- Configuration item identifier: name–type–version.
- Original author.
- Creation date.
- Change history: version–date–author–description.

Another **essential** property of an effective configuration management system is the clear labelling of all documentation and storage media in a standard format. Whatever format is used, it should contain at least the following **essential** details:

- Project name.
- Configuration item identifier: name–type–version.
- Date.
- Content description.

Configuration Item Storage

Configuration items are usually stored in a software library. A software library can be described as a controlled collection of configuration items and can exist on various media, such as disk, tape or paper. At a minimum, the following set of software libraries is **essential** to ensure adequate security and control of all deliverable software items:

Library Type	Description
Development library	Dynamic
Master library	Controlled
Static library	Static

Development library. This is a dynamic library, where software is coded and tested as a set of modules.

Master library. A master library is a controlled library where items can enter or leave only under prescribed and controlled conditions. After successful unit testing, modules are transferred to a master library for integration and system testing. Any modules requiring modification as a result of this testing are transferred back to the development library for the changes to be carried out.

Static library. When a master library has reached a reasonable state of stability, it can then be incorporated into a baseline. Whenever such a baseline is released, copies of all the master libraries which it incorporates are taken. These copies, known as static libraries because they are never modified, are then archived to provide a physical 'audit trail' of software development baselines.

It is **essential** to manage these libraries so that:

- procedures for regular backup of development libraries are established;
- static libraries are never, under any circumstances, modified;
- up-to-date security copies of all master and static libraries are always available.

Configuration Change Control

Software configuration control of an item can only occur after the item has been formally identified and incorporated into a baseline, and has two main aspects:

- evaluating proposed changes to configuration items;
- coordinating approved changes.

These demand the definition of methods for handling change proposals, and for altering the level of authority required to change each item. As a configuration item passes through unit, integration, system and acceptance testing, a higher level of authority should be required to approve changes.

When a software item does not conform to its specification, it is **essential** to identify it as non-conforming and to hold it for review action. The non-conformance is then classified as major or minor, depending on its level of severity and urgency.

Problem Reporting and Corrective Action

Problems can occur at any stage in the evolution of a software system and can be placed in one of the following categories:

- Operations error.
- Documentation does not conform to code.
- Code does not conform to design.
- Design does not conform to requirements.
- New or changed requirements.

The phase of the life cycle at which corrective action must start is determined by which of the above categories best describes the problem. In some cases, the problem may not be discovered until a later phase of the development than that in which it occurs. Backtracking through the life cycle is then necessary to ensure that corrections are carried out.

Appropriate procedures for handling problem reports and change proposals are **essential**. It is **essential** for these procedures to adequately cover the logging, analysis, decision and follow-up of problems, by requiring that:

- A software problem report is completed for each problem detected, giving all relevent information about the symptoms and circumstances of the problem.
- The software problem report is passed to an appropriate body, which assigns it to the relevant authority for analysis. Following analysis, a software change request may be generated, which outlines all changes necessary to rectify the problem.
- An appropriate body reviews the software change request and, if accepted, assigns someone to carry out the changes.
- Each completed modification is recorded on a software modification report.

Documentation Change Procedures

It is **essential** to establish appropriate procedures for reviewing and approving documents and changes to documents (including procedures, plans, and product-related documents). These procedures must also ensure that pertinent issues of documents are available for use where and when required. It is **important** for these procedures to ensure that:

- A draft of the document is produced and submitted for review. All changed text should be marked if the document is not new.
- The reviewers record their comments about the document on document review reports, including any recommended changes or solutions.
- The author(s) of the document examine each document review report and record their response on the report.
- Each document review report is then processed at a formal review meeting.
- The draft document and the approved document review reports are used to generate the next revision of the document. If there are major changes, a new issue is released.
- Each revision or issue of a document is accompanied by a document change record, outlining the changes that have been made.

Configuration Status Accounting

Configuration status accounting involves the tracking and reporting of all configuration items and is conducted throughout the life cycle. It is therefore **essential** to record the status of all configuration items.

In order to perform configuration status accounting effectively, it is **essential** to record the following information on each project:

- The date, version and issue of each baseline.
- The date and status of each document review report and document change record.
- The date and status of each software problem report, software change request and software modification report.
- Summary descriptions of each configuration item.

Release

It is **essential** to document the first release of the software in a software transfer document, and to accompany subsequent releases with a software release note. This note lists the configuration items in the release and the procedures for installing them. In addition, it is **essential** to record in the note all faults that have been repaired and any new requirements that have been incorporated.

It is **essential** to re-test all modified software before release. It is also **essential**, for each release, to ensure that documentation is consistent with code and that previous releases are archived.

7.3.3 Coverage of Configuration Management Plans

Configuration management plans are concerned with establishing a structure for controlling and coordinating the key software items of a project. It is **essential** to document these plans, giving adequate coverage to the following areas:

Introduction

- Purpose.
- Scope.

Configuration Identification

- Code control.
- Media control.
- Software tool control.
- Change control.
- Problem reporting.

Configuration Status Accounting

Software Configuration Tools, Techniques and Methods

Supplier Control

Records Collection and Retention

7.3.4   Evolution of Configuration Management Plans

It is **essential** to plan and establish appropriate configuration management procedures for controlling all key software items (that is requirements, designs, code and documentation) throughout the project. It is **important** for configuration management procedures to be simple and efficient, and to be reused in later project phases whenever appropriate. Outline plans are produced at the start of the project and are refined into detailed plans for each phase. The evolution of configuration management plans is outlined below:

User requirements. User requirements configuration management plans describe or reference configuration management procedures for all documentation produced during the user requirements phase.

Software requirements. Software requirements configuration management plans define configuration management procedures for all documentation and tool outputs (for example data flow diagrams) produced during the phase. If prototyping is used to clarify or extract specific software requirements, configuration management procedures covering the prototype code are included.

Architectural design. Configuration management plans for the architectural design phase describe in detail configuration management procedures for all documentation and tool outputs for the phase. If prototyping is to be used to examine specific aspects of a possible design solution, configuration management procedures for the prototype code are also included. Unless tool outputs or prototype code differ significantly in nature from those used in the software requirements phase, the same configuration management procedures are reused.

Production. Production phase configuration management plans define configuration management procedures for maintaining all documentation, deliverable code, tool outputs and prototype code under configuration management. Unless there is good reason not to, architectural design phase procedures are reused.

Transfer. Transfer phase configuration management plans define procedures for the configuration management of all deliverables in the operational environment, for the duration of the transfer phase.

Maintenance. Configuration management procedures are as important for the maintenance phase as for any other phase. Between provisional and final acceptance, transfer phase configuration management plans can be used. However, these plans need to be reviewed after final acceptance, and periodically thereafter, to ensure they remain effective.

7.4   Verification

7.4.1   Purpose

Verification is essential for ensuring the quality of a product and is both a managerial and a technical function. Verification is formally defined in the IEEE 729 standard as:

> 'the act of reviewing, inspecting, testing, checking, auditing, or otherwise establishing and documenting whether or not items, processes, services or documents conform to specified requirements.'

A corollary to verification is validation, which can be defined as:

> 'the evaluation of software throughout the software development process to ensure compliance with user requirements.'

Verification then, is about answering the question, 'Am I building the product correctly?', while validation is about answering the question, 'Am I building the correct product?'.

7.4.2   Activities

Verification can sometimes prove to be the most expensive and time-consuming part of a project. However, it is **essential** for verification activities to reflect the criticality and required quality of the software. These activities include:

• reviews of all key items and deliverables;
• checking the traceability of software requirements to user requirements;
• checking the traceability of design components to software requirements;

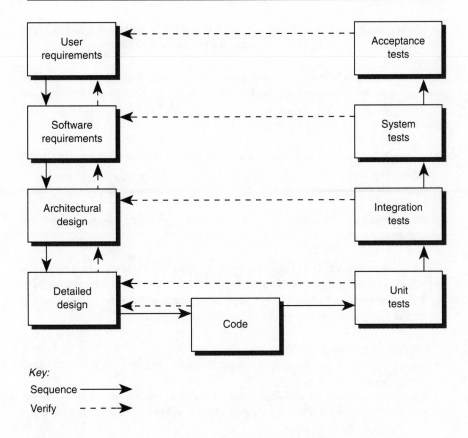

Figure 7.2 Overview of verification through the life cycle.

- checking formal proofs and algorithms;
- unit, integration, system and acceptance testing;
- selective auditing of key software items.

Reviews

A software review is an evaluation of a software element to ascertain discrepancies from planned results and to recommend improvements. Three different types of review are useful for software verification:

- Walkthrough.
- Software inspection.
- Technical review.

Walkthroughs. Walkthroughs provide an **important** means of early evaluation of documents, models, designs and code. The objective of a walkthrough is to evaluate a specific software element with a view to identifying defects and considering possible solutions.

Software inspections. It is **important** to use software inspections for evaluation of documents and code prior to technical review or testing. A software inspection is intended to be a rigorous peer examination, the objective of which is to:

- identify points of non-conformance with respect to specifications and standards;
- measure progress.

Stylistic issues should be ignored and solutions should not be discussed.

Technical reviews. It is **important** to subject all major software items produced during a phase to a technical review before they are signed off. The objective of such a review is to evaluate a specific software element with a view to providing evidence that it:

- conforms to specification;
- was produced according to appropriate project standards and procedures;
- has been subject to change control so that all changes have been properly implemented and only affect system areas identified in the change specification.

Tracing

Each input to a phase must be matched to an output of the same phase to demonstrate completeness. This is called 'forwards traceability'. It is usually performed by constructing cross-reference matrices for the inputs and outputs. Holes in the matrices indicate incompleteness.

Backwards traceability is complementary to forwards traceability and requires that each output of a phase is traceable to an input of the phase. Assuming that the inputs to the phase are complete, outputs which cannot be traced back to an input are superfluous.

During the life cycle, it is **important** to verify the backwards and forwards traceability of the following groups of items:

- User requirements and software requirements.
- Software requirements and component descriptions.
- Integration tests and major design components.
- System tests and software requirements.
- Acceptance tests and user requirements.

Testing

Testing is the process of exercising or evaluating a system or system component, by manual or automated means, to:

- confirm that it satisfies specified requirements;
- identify differences between expected and actual results.

The expense of testing software is frequently underestimated, and increases with the number of errors present before it commences. Research has shown that it frequently accounts for up to 50% of project cost. It is therefore **essential** to apply cheaper methods of removing errors, such as inspections and walkthroughs, before testing is started. It is **essential** to analyze records of defects, to identify the causes of defects, and to take action to eliminate them. It is **essential** to produce the following documents for all unit, integration, system and acceptance testing activities:

Phase / Tests	User Requirements	Software Requirements	Architectural Requirements	Production	Transfer
Acceptance Tests	Plans			• Designs • Cases • Procedures	Reports
System Tests		Plans		• Designs • Cases • Procedures • Reports	
Integration Tests			Plans	• Designs • Cases • Procedures • Reports	
Unit Tests				• Plans • Designs • Cases • Procedures • Reports	

Figure 7.3 Production of test documentation.

- Outline plan describing the general testing approach and resources.
- Detailed test design describing the different kinds of test that will be performed.
- Test case specification defining the inputs, expected results and execution conditions of each test.
- Test procedure specification stating the sequence of actions to be carried out by test personnel.
- Test report describing the execution of the test procedures.

Auditing

Audits are independent reviews that assess compliance with specification, standards and procedures. A physical audit checks that all items identified as being part of the configuration are present; a functional audit checks that unit, integration and system tests have been carried out and records their success or failure. It is **essential** to perform physical and functional audits before each software release.

Coverage of Verification Plans

Verification plans deal with establishing standards and procedures through which it can be verified that a given software item conforms to specified requirements. It is **essential** to document these plans, with at least the following level of detail:

Purpose

Reference Documents

Verification Overview

- Organization.
- Master schedule.
- Resources summary.
- Responsibilities.
- Tools, techniques and methods.

Verification Administrative Procedures

- Anomaly reporting and resolution.
- Deviation policy.
- Control procedures.
- Standards, practices and conventions.

Verification Activities

- Requirements traceability.
- Formal proofs.
- Reviews.
- Subcontracted work.
- Third party software.

Testing Activities

- Plans.
- Designs.
- Test cases.
- Procedures.
- Reports.

Software Verification Reporting

7.4.4 Evolution of Verification Plans

As in configuration management, it is **essential** to subject all key software items to verification, to ensure that they conform to specification and that all stated user requirements are engineered into the design and code of the software. It is **essential** to produce documented plans for verification activities, which ensure that the verification activities:

- are appropriate for the degree of criticality of the software;
- meet the verification and acceptance testing requirements stated in the software requirements document;
- verify that the product meets the quality, reliability, maintainability and safety requirements stated in the software requirements document;
- are sufficient to ensure the quality of the software in general.

Outline plans are produced at the start of the project and are refined into detailed plans for each phase. The evolution of verification plans is described below.

User requirements. Verification plans for the user requirements phase define the review procedures by which the user requirements document will be evaluated. An **essential** part of these plans is the acceptance test plan, which defines the approach, scope, resources and schedule of the acceptance testing activities.

Software requirements. Software requirements verification plans outline, among other things, the methods by which user requirements will be traced to software requirements. A description of the review procedures by which the software requirements document will be evaluated is also a part of the plans. An **essential** part of the software requirements verification plans is the system test plan, which outlines the approach, resources and schedule for system testing activities.

Architectural design. Verification plans for the architectural design phase define the methods by which software requirements can be traced to design components. These plans also describe how the architectural design will be verified by defining the design review procedures and evaluation criteria. The integration test plan is an **essential** part of the architectural design verification plans, and describes the approach, scope, resources and schedule of the integration tests.

Production. Verification plans for the production phase describe how the detailed design and code are to be evaluated by defining the review and traceability procedures. As detailed design and coding information become available during the production stage itself, it is **essential** to develop unit test plans, outlining the approach, scope, resources and schedule of the intended unit tests.

Transfer. Transfer phase verification plans describe the review procedures by which all deliverables will be evaluated.

Maintenance. Verification plans for the maintenance phase describe review and traceability procedures for the evaluation of code fixes and modifications. Substantial enhancements should be treated as separate projects in their own right.

7.5   Software Quality Assurance (SQA)

7.5.1 Purpose

Software Quality Assurance is a planned and systematic pattern of actions to provide adequate confidence that the item or product conforms to established technical requirements. In a more specific project context, it is about ensuring that project standards and procedures are adequate to provide the required degree of quality, and that they are adhered to throughout the project.

It is **essential** for quality assurance activities to be carried out by independent staff. On small projects, quality assurance can be performed by staff from other projects. For larger projects, it is **important** to allocate specific staff to this role.

7.5.2 Activities

Management

Analysis of the managerial structure that influences and controls the quality of the software is an SQA activity. It is **essential** for an appropriate structure to be in place and for individuals within the structure to have clearly defined tasks and responsibilities.

Documentation

It is **essential** to analyze the documentation plan for the project, to identify deviations from standards relating to such plans, and to discuss these with project management.

Standards and Practices

It is **essential** to monitor adherence to all standards and practices throughout the project.

Reviews and Audits

It is **essential** to examine project review and audit arrangements, to ensure that they are adequate and to verify that they are appropriate for the type of project. To this end, it is **useful** for SQA personnel to attend a sample of reviews.

Testing

Unit, integration, system and acceptance testing of executable software are an integral part of the development of quality software. It is therefore **essential** to review all plans or reports connected with these activities, such as test plans, test designs, test cases, test procedures and test reports.

Problem Reporting and Corrective Action

It is **essential** to review and monitor project error-handling proce-dures to ensure that problems are reported and tracked from identification right through to resolution, and that problem causes are eliminated where possible. It is also **important** to monitor the execution of these procedures and examine trends in problem occurrence.

Tools, Techniques and Methods

Tools, techniques and methods for software production should be defined at the project level. It is **important** to check the appropriateness of these methods and tools, and to monitor their correct application throughout the project. In cases where additional tools or techniques are necessary to support this monitoring activity, these should be documented.

Code and Media Control

It is **essential** to check that the procedures, methods and facilities used to maintain, store, secure and document controlled versions of software are adequate and are used properly.

Supplier Control

It is **essential** to check software acquired from external suppliers against project standards. It is **essential** to require each sub-contractor to produce a software quality assurance plan which can be checked and validated.

Records Collection, Maintenance and Retention

In addition to the documentation required of any software project, additional documents such as minutes of meetings and review records are also produced. It is **essential** to ensure that adequate methods and facilities exist to assemble, safeguard and maintain all this additional documentation, at least for the life-span of the project. These records are required both to give evidence of adherence to prescribed procedures and standards, and for later analysis aimed at process improvement.

Training

It is **essential** to ensure that all development staff are appropriately skilled for their tasks and to identify any training required to bring this about.

Risk Management

Project managers must identify and control the factors critical to project success. Although this risk management is primarily a project management activity, it is **important** to monitor risk management activities, and to advise project management on appropriate methods and procedures for identifying, assessing and controlling the areas of risk.

7.5.3 Structure of Quality Assurance Plans

Quality assurance plans are concerned with defining the means by which the degree of adherence to, and adequacy of, project standards and procedures can be independently and objectively determined. It is **essential** to document these plans, with adequate coverage of the areas outlined below. In some cases, the plans may duplicate or overlap other plans. In such cases, it is sufficient to simply reference the procedures concerned, rather than document them repeatedly.

Purpose

Reference Documents

Management

Documentation

Standards, Practices, Conventions and Metrics
- Documentation standards.
- Design standards.
- Coding standards.
- Code commenting standards.
- Testing standards and practices.
- Software quality assurance metrics.
- Compliance monitoring.

Reviews and Audits

Tests

Problem Reporting and Corrective Action

Tools, Techniques and Methods

Code Control

Media Control

Supplier Control

Records Collection, Maintenance and Retention

Training

Risk Management

7.5.4   Evolution of Quality Assurance Plans

Like all other major project plans, an outline plan is produced at the start of the project and later refined into detailed plans for each phase. The evolution of quality assurance plans is summarized below:

User requirements. User requirements quality assurance plans describe in detail the quality assurance activities to be carried out during the phase.

Software requirements. Quality assurance plans for the software requirements phase describe the quality assurance activities for the phase.

Architectural design. Quality assurance plans for the architectural design phase detail the quality assurance activities for the phase.

Production. Production phase quality assurance plans describe the quality assurance activities for the production phase.

Transfer. Quality assurance plans for the transfer phase cover quality assurance activities during the installation and transfer of the software.

Maintenance. Quality assurance plans for the maintenance phase describe the quality assurance activities for the maintenance phase. Since this phase potentially can last indefinitely, these plans must be periodically reviewed and updated to remain effective.

8
Organization Level Activities

Chapters 6 and 7 identified life cycle and supporting activities that should be introduced in every software development or maintenance project. However, these are not sufficient to ensure consistently high performance on all projects: to provide proper control across all projects, the software organization must also introduce activities, relating to the organization as a whole, which cover:

- Process Management.
- Procurement.
- Training.
- Management Responsibility.

8.1   Process Management

Software development can be extremely complex, and frequently there are alternative ways to perform a given task. A defined software process provides a framework within which staff can make choices in an orderly way. Such a framework improves communication between staff, allows them to be moved quickly and easily between projects, and makes planning more reliable. However, software engineering is not an activity that can be rigidly regimented and structured like a repetitive manufacturing process. There is therefore a need to trade off the individual project's need for flexibility against the benefits of defined standards and procedures to the organization. The aim should be to:

- define a standard software process;
- ensure that each project uses an appropriate version of the standard process that has been tailored to its individual needs;
- use the results from projects to improve the standard process.

The software organization must establish functions to manage the defined process, and in particular, to carry out process measurement, process improvement and technology innovation activities. In a large organization, these functions may be discharged by one or more dedicated teams. In smaller organizations, they may be part-time responsibilities, or, in the smallest organizations, a director may be nominated to discharge them, assembling an ad-hoc team to do so as required.

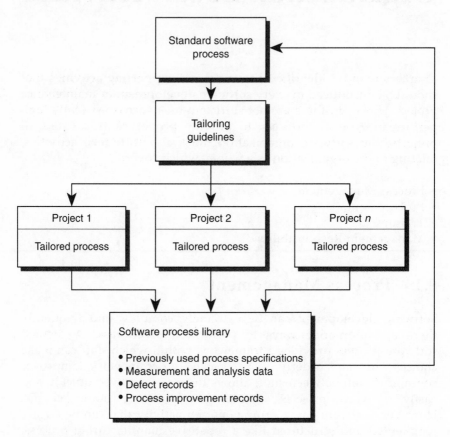

Figure 8.1 Overview of Process Management activities.

8.1.1 Defining a Standard Process

It is **essential** to establish and maintain a documented standard software process for the organization, which may be tailored to projects' individual needs. It is **important** for staff and managers involved in implementing the process to participate in the definition of it, and to be kept informed about it. Defining a standard software process is a significant task, so it is **important** to carry out the definition activities in accordance with a documented plan. This plan must set out the activities and schedule for defining the process, specify group and individual responsibilities for the activities, and identify the required resources. It is **important** for management to review and approve the plan before it is implemented.

It is **important** for the standard process to reflect any constraints on working practice that may be imposed by customers, and for it to incorporate up-to-date software engineering methods and tools. It is also **important** to ensure that it makes provision for the collection of project measurements (see Section 8.1.4). The standard process describes and orders the software tasks that are common to all projects. It also contains guidelines for tailoring the standard process to the needs of different projects, so that each project has its own approved life cycle which defines:

• Required procedures, practices, methods and technologies.
• Applicable process and product standards.
• Responsibilities, authorities and staff interrelationships.
• Required tools and resources.
• Process dependencies and interfaces.
• Process outputs and completion criteria.
• Product and process measurements to be collected.

8.1.2 Improving the Standard Process

Process improvement is about continually improving the organization's defined software process and the project processes that are derived from it. This involves identifying, evaluating and implementing improvements to the standard process. Improvements can be identified by monitoring, measuring and reviewing the performance of the standard process as it is applied in individual projects. It is **important** to ensure that staff and managers who are involved in using the software process participate in the process improvement activities, and it is **essential** to keep them informed about them.

It is **important** to set and track quantitative, measurable goals for process improvement, and to direct these goals at increasing product quality and productivity (see Section 8.1.4). A process improvement programme should be established that empowers staff and managers to improve their own working processes and participate in improvements made by others. In initiating such a programme, it is **useful** to establish a function to manage and support process improvement, and to establish programmes and activities that encourage staff to submit improvement proposals. It is **essential** for such programmes to include a process for submitting, reviewing, approving and implementing improvement proposals. It is also

important to give appropriate recognition to staff who originate good proposals.

It is **important** to prepare and maintain plans for process improvement covering the whole organization. These plans should define the required resources, staffing and tools, identify the highest priority areas for process improvement, and specify goals for process performance improvement. They should also identify and assign teams to address improvements for specific areas. Examples of such teams include working groups, quality circles, and technical committees.

8.1.3 Process Record Keeping

An **important** tool in monitoring the software process is to maintain a library of software process information and make it available for use by individual projects. The process specifications tailored for use by previous projects are a **useful** part of such a library. If they are included, it is **important** to control and maintain them, and to include only suitable process specifications from previous projects. It is also **important** to review the reuse of each process specification periodically.

An **essential** element of the library is information about the outcome of completed projects. This includes lessons learned from previous projects, and measurements to be used for calibrating models for estimating software size and costs. To ensure the integrity of such information, it is **essential** to review it before it is entered into the library.

8.1.4 Measuring the Software Process

It is **essential** to take measurements of the performance of the standard software process, as applied by individual projects, and to analyze these measurements. It is **essential** to use the analysis to adjust the standard process, with a view to improving it and stabilizing its performance within acceptable limits.

A **useful** way of introducing process measurement is to set up a function in the organization which focuses specifically on process measurement and analysis. It is **important** to involve quality assurance staff and software managers in measurement activities, and ensure that they have appropriate tools to collect, store, validate, analyze and report measurement data.

It is **important** to drive process measurement and analysis activities from a documented and approved plan. This plan should specify the goals and objectives of the measurement programme. The objectives should be tied to the organization's strategic product quality and productivity goals. The plan should also describe and schedule the activities to be performed, identify the groups and individuals responsible for the activities, specify the required resources, staffing and tools, and identify the procedures to be followed.

In developing a measurement and analysis programme, the following issues need to be resolved:

- What should be measured?
- Why it should be measured?
- How it should be measured?
- Who should measure it?
- When and where in the process it should be measured?

It is **essential** to link the selected process and product metrics to your ability to meet your customers' requirements. While some measurements may primarily benefit the organization and the individual project, you must optimize the process to meeting customers' requirements. The selected metrics should therefore:

- be linked to real customer requirements;
- support the overall goals and objectives of the measurement programme;
- support predefined analysis activities;
- be consistent across all projects;
- cover the entire life cycle, including support and maintenance.

Examples of specific measurements that can be used are:

- estimated versus actual size, cost and schedule data;
- quality measurements as defined in the quality plan;
- number and severity of defects in requirements, design and code;
- number and cost of changes to approved requirements and design specifications;
- number and turnaround time of customer requests and fault reports.

It is **important** to prepare reports of process measurements and to distribute them regularly to appropriate groups and individuals.

8.1.5 Defect Prevention

Defect prevention is concerned with ensuring that sources of defects that are inherent in the software process, or of defects that occur repeatedly, are identified and eliminated. Defect prevention activities should be defined and implemented at both organizational and project level, and these activities should be appropriately coordinated at each level.

At the project level, it is **essential** to include defect prevention activities in the project development plan and schedule. One **useful** technique is to hold meetings during the development to identify defects and analyze their root causes. The defects can then be categorized by cause, such as inadequate training, breakdown of communications, oversight of important details, or manual errors (for example typing mistakes). When defects have been identified and classified, measures to prevent their recurrence can be developed and documented. Such measures can include changes to the software process, the training programme, the tools and methods used or the communication procedures between groups and individuals. Records of causal analysis meetings should be kept for use by the organization and by future projects.

At the level of the organization, it is **essential** to identify and document trends which indicate broad problems across several projects, and to take corrective action to eliminate them. An **essential** part of the defect prevention programme is to follow up and coordinate defect prevention activities across the organization, to ensure that they take place and have the desired effect. It can be **useful** to record information on proposed defect prevention actions, such as the:

- description of the defect;
- description of the cause;
- category of the cause;
- stage where the defect was introduced;
- stage where the defect was identified;
- description of the proposed action;
- person responsible for implementing the action;
- description of the areas affected by the action;
- individuals who are kept informed of the action's status;
- date of the next status review;
- rationale for key decisions.

It is **important** for software engineering staff and managers to receive feedback on the status and results of the defect prevention activities on a regular basis. This feedback should provide a summary of the major defect categories, the frequency distribution of defects in each major category, and details on significant innovations and actions taken to address the major defect categories.

8.1.6   Technology Innovation

It is **essential** to monitor and evaluate new technologies, and to implement them as appropriate within the organization. It is therefore **important** for the organization to develop and maintain a plan for technology innovation. This plan should define the organization's long-term technical strategy for automating and improving software process activities, and describe its plans for introducing new technologies. It should identify process areas that are potential areas for technology innovation, and also identify candidate tools and technologies.

It is **important** to incorporate selected new technologies into the organization's standard software process in a controlled and orderly way. This means that the resources required to install, maintain and support the technology must be established before the technology is introduced. A strategy should be developed for measuring process performance in the light of the new technology. It is **important** to identify technology changes that clearly affect process stability, and to revise the standard process specifications to incorporate the new technologies. It is **important** for staff and managers to receive regular feedback on the status of new technologies and the results that have been achieved by their use, and for them to be kept aware of relevant areas where new tools and technologies have been used successfully.

It is **useful** as part of the technology innovation programme to establish a specific function with responsibility for technology innovation, coordinating innovation activities, providing assistance to others who are exploring potential areas for innovation and selecting and planning new technologies.

8.1.7 Process Change Management

It is **essential** to maintain the organization's standard software process under configuration management. It is therefore **essential** to document and review changes derived from the following sources, and for management to approve such changes:

- Findings and recommendations of process audits and assessments.
- Lessons learned from monitoring process activities.
- Change proposals from project staff and managers.
- Analyzed and interpreted process and product measurement data.

It is **essential** to establish and follow procedures for planning, approving, implementing, reviewing and tracking process improvement proposals. These procedures should ensure that:

- Each proposal is evaluated, and the reasons for accepting or rejecting it documented.
- The expected benefits of each process improvement are defined.
- The priority of selected improvement proposals is determined.

- Implementation of proposals is assigned and planned.
- The status of each proposal is tracked.
- Checks are made that completed improvement actions have had the desired effect before closure.
- Submitters of proposals are informed of any decisions regarding their proposals.

Where appropriate, it can be **useful** to implement process improvements on a pilot basis to determine their benefits and effectiveness before introducing them on a broad scale.

It is **important** to track change activity for the standard process, to determine if it is stable.

8.1.8   Reviewing the Software Process

It is **essential** to review the status, adequacy and efficiency of the standard software process periodically (at least annually).

It is **essential** to define clearly the responsibilities for these reviews, to assign them to designated managers or staff, and to keep records of them.

8.2   Procurement

It is **essential** for the organization to develop and maintain procedures in relation to the procurement of key inputs to the software process, and in particular, to the purchasing and subcontracting of software.

In the case of subcontracted software, it is **essential** to ensure that the subcontract software standards, procedures and product requirements comply with the prime contractor's commitments, and that the prime contractor tracks the subcontractor's actual results and performance against them.

It is **essential** to select suppliers on the basis of their ability to meet stated requirements, to keep records of their performance, and to use these records, when available, for supplier selection.

It is **essential** to verify supplies on receipt, to ensure that they meet stated requirements. This includes items supplied by the customer.

It is **important** to establish a contractual agreement between the prime contractor and the subcontractor, and to make this the basis for managing the subcontract. The contractual agreement should include or reference the contract terms and conditions, and a work statement. The work statement defines the scope of the work, the technical goals and objectives, and any imposed standards and procedures. It also specifies any cost, schedule or other development constraints. The contractual agreement should also reference the requirements specification for any contracted deliverables, and the acceptance procedures and criteria applied to them.

It is **important** for the prime contractor to review and approve the subcontractor's software development plan, and to use this for tracking the software activities and status of the subcontract. It is also **important** to conduct formal reviews at selected milestones of the subcontract to address the subcontractor's software engineering accomplishments and results.

It is **essential** to evaluate the subcontractor's performance on a periodic basis and to record the results of such evaluations.

8.3   Training

It is **essential** for the organization to develop training programmes to ensure that staff and managers have the skills and knowledge to perform their jobs effectively. It is also **essential** to review the training programmes periodically, and to revise them as necessary.

An important element is an organization training plan which is reviewed periodically. This plan should identify the skills needed and when they are required. It should also define the resources necessary to conduct or procure relevant training courses.

It is **essential** for each project to develop and maintain a training plan which identifies the set of skills needed within the project and its training needs. It may be necessary to develop, maintain and conduct training courses at the project level.

It is **essential** for records of training to be maintained and used by management. These records should detail staff training histories and courses which have been successfully completed.

8.4   Management Responsibility

It is **essential** for management to define and document its policy, objectives and commitment to quality, and to ensure that they are understood and implemented at all levels in the organization.

It is **essential** to define the responsibility, authority and interrelation of all staff who manage, perform and verify work affecting quality.

It is **essential** for management, at regular intervals, to formally review the arrangements they have established to ensure quality (usually called the quality system), to ensure their continuing effectiveness and efficiency. It is **essential** to document this management review. Management review should not duplicate any other review and monitoring activities which may have been established, but draw on their results. It must cover:

- Organization and responsibilities.
- Authorized procedures.
- The standard software process and the associated measurement programme.
- Feedback from customers, including customer complaints.
- The performance of suppliers.
- The effectiveness of corrective action and defect prevention mechanisms.
- The results of internal quality audits.

Appendix A
The ISO 9000 Series of International Standards and their Use for Software

A.1 The ISO 9000 Series

ISO 9000 is a series of quality systems standards and associated guidance material first published in 1987 by the International Standards Organization (ISO). The European Committee for Standardization (CEN) has adopted the series, giving it Euro Norm numbers in the EN 29000 range. It is now implemented under CEN rules and without alteration as national standards in all CEN member states. One hundred and thirty seven countries are currently using the identical standards as national standards and three further countries use equivalent standards. They can be obtained from the national standards body in each country that has adopted them, or from ISO Headquarters in Geneva.

Appropriate standards from the series are selected to meet the needs of different industries. For the software industry, the appropriate standards are:

- ISO 9001:1987/EN 29001 Quality Systems – Model for Quality Assurance in Design/Development, Production, Installation and Servicing. This standard applies to all products and services where meeting technical requirements involves design. It is used as the prime standard for assessment, supported by the following guidelines where appropriate.

- ISO 9000–3 Guidelines for the Application of ISO 9001 to the Development, Supply and Maintenance of Software. This tailors ISO 9001 for use in the software industry.

- ISO 9004–2 Quality Management and Quality Systems Elements – Part 2: Guidelines for Services. This gives guidelines for service quality, which are applicable to support services associated with software products.

An additional standard, recently published, which may be useful is:

- ISO 9004–4 Quality Management and Quality System Elements – Part 4: Guidelines for Quality Improvement.

There are two further standards for assessment. ISO 9002 is applicable where no design is necessary to meet technical requirements. It may be used instead of ISO 9001 as the prime standard for some suppliers of software-related services which involve no design. Examples would include some consultancy, computer training, and service bureau firms. ISO 9003 is applicable to assembly and test operations, but is no longer used.

Note that ISO 9001, 9002, and 9003 are in the process of being updated. The revised documents are currently at Draft International Standard status, and are likely to become full standards during 1994. Any changes are likely to be minor.

A.2   Overview of ISO 9001

ISO 9001 concisely lists requirements to be met by a quality system for use when conformance to specified requirements is to be assured during several stages, which may include design/development, production, installation and servicing. The emphasis is on operating suitable management controls. The flavour is that of manufacturing industry, but it is possible with some careful thought to interpret the requirements in a way appropriate to software development and support. ISO 9000–3 does this.

The requirements are grouped under 20 headings:

Management responsibility	Inspection measuring and test equipment
Quality system	Inspection and test status
Contract review	Control of non-conforming product
Design control	
Document control	Corrective action
Purchasing	Handling, storage, packaging and delivery
Purchaser supplied product	
Product identification and traceability	Quality records
	Internal quality audits
Process control	Training
Inspection and testing	Servicing
	Statistical techniques

A.3   Overview of ISO 9000–3

ISO 9000–3 sets out guidelines to facilitate the application of ISO 9001 to organizations developing, supplying and maintaining software. It splits the subject matter into three broad categories that need to be addressed in establishing a quality system: the overall Framework, the Life Cycle Activities, and the Supporting Activities, which complete and integrate the overall system.

A.3.1 Framework

The framework deals with questions of management responsibility, the quality system, internal quality system audits, and corrective action.

Management Responsibility

This covers the supplier's management responsibilities for quality policy, establishing clear responsibilities, authorities and lines of communication, providing adequate resources and personnel for verification activities, and reviewing the suitability of the quality system regularly. It also covers the customer's responsibility to cooperate with the supplier and take part in joint reviews.

The Quality System

This covers establishing and maintaining a quality system which is integrated into all aspects of the business.

Internal Quality System Audits

These ensure that the quality system is effective.

Corrective Action

This covers establishing procedures to deal with non-conformance of product or process.

A.3.2 Life Cycle Activities

All aspects of the life cycle need to be addressed. In particular the standard draws attention to:

Contract reviews	Design and implementation
Purchasing requirements	Testing and validation
Development planning	Acceptance procedures
Quality planning	Maintenance procedures

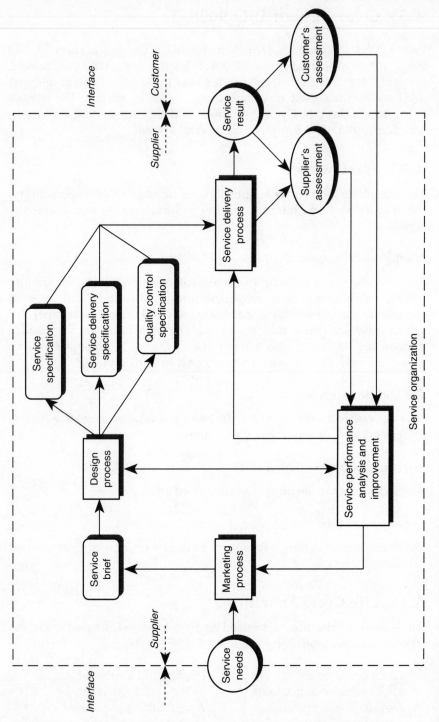

Figure A1. Service quality loop (after ISO 9004.2).

A.3.3 Supporting Activities

This covers activities that must be addressed throughout the life cycle, such as:

Configuration management	Tools and techniques
Document control	Purchasing
Quality records	Inclusion of external software
Measurements	products
Rules, practices and	Training
conventions	

A.4 ISO 9004-2

ISO 9004–2 gives guidance for establishing and implementing a quality system in an organization that provides services to customers, with or without a degree of product content. As such it is applicable to software organizations that support the products they supply. The concepts and principles are applicable to both large and small organizations, although small organizations will not have, nor need, the complex structure necessary in the larger enterprise.

The standard identifies a number of quality system principles which must be built into a suitable quality system:

- Management is responsible for quality policy and objectives, for ensuring defined responsibilities, authorities and lines of communication, and for management review.
- Management must plan to provide sufficient and appropriate resources to implement the quality system and achieve the quality objectives, including trained personnel and material resources.
- The quality system must be set up to provide adequate control over all operational processes affecting quality, and must emphasize preventive action without sacrificing the ability to respond to and correct failures as they arise.
- Steps must be taken to establish effective interaction between customers and the service organization's personnel, which is crucial to the quality of service perceived by the customer.

The standard uses the idea of a service quality loop to describe the operational elements of a service quality system, and specifies what is required under the following headings:

- Marketing process.
- Design process.

- Service delivery process.
- Service performance analysis and improvement.

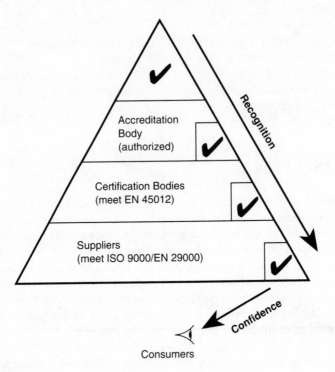

Figure A2.

A.5   Use of the Standards

The ISO 9000 standards may be used to assess the suitability of an organization's quality system in three different modes:

- First Party Assessment, carried out by the organization itself. This can be very useful to the organization as part of a quality improvement initiative, but lacks credibility with customers.
- Second Party Assessment, carried out by individual customers to assure themselves of the organization's capability. This is costly for both customers and the organization because assessments are duplicated.
- Third Party Assessment, carried out by an independent body.

The term ISO 9000 certification is generally used to describe third party assessment against appropriate ISO 9000 standards, accompanied by some scheme to publicize a successful result, such as by inclusion on a register, or by awarding a certificate. Where the main standard used for assessment is ISO 9001 (as for software) the term ISO 9001 certification is often used.

A.6   Accreditation

ISO 9000 certification is only of use if the independent body carrying it out is recognized in the industry as reputable and objective. The purpose of accreditation is to promote this, and ensure that different certification bodies' assessments against ISO 9000 have the same meaning.

Accreditation is a process in which recognition of competence is passed down in a controlled way from a government (or other authoritative body) to a supplier, and made visible to customers. Recognition of competence is often symbolized by a mark of recognition or a logo. An accreditation body is established with suitable authority, typically by a government. The accreditation body accredits a certification body after satisfying itself that the certification body operates in accordance with appropriate criteria of competence, thereby passing recognition on to the certification body. The certification body in turn certifies suppliers, and passes recognition on to them. Consumers can then look for suppliers recognized in this way, with confidence that their quality system meets appropriate best practice criteria.

In Europe, accreditation bodies use Euro Norm EN 45012 General Criteria for Certification Bodies Operating Quality Management Certification as criteria of competence, together with other national criteria to meet the local needs of industry, government and commerce.

Accreditation schemes typically require that certification bodies themselves have an effective quality system, and that in particular:

- Assessors are appropriately qualified,
- Assessors work to equivalent guidelines, in addition to ISO 9000,
- The scope and frequency of assessment and surveillance meet minimum standards.

Appendix B
Additional Background and Reference Material

General Quality References

Crosby P. (1978). *Quality is Free.* Maidenhead: McGraw Hill

NSAI *ISO 9000 Series of Standards.* EOLAS, Glasnevin, Dublin 9 (or other ISO National Member Body)

Oakland J.S. (1989). *Total Quality Management.* Heinemann Professional Publishing

PA Consulting Group (1988). *The Total Quality Experience: A Guide for the continuing journey.* PA Consulting Group, 10/12 Landsdowne Road, Ballsbridge, Dublin 4.

Peters T. (1988). *Thriving on Chaos.* London: Collier Macmillan

Quinn F. (1990). *Crowning the Customer.* O'Brien Press

Rothery B. (1993). *ISO 9000* 2nd edn. Aldershot: Gower

Smith S. (1986). *How to Take Part in the Quality Revolution: A Management Guide* PA Consulting Group, 10/12 Landsdowne Road, Ballsbridge, Dublin 4. 1986

Software Quality References

Bryan W. L. (1988). *Software Product Assurance: Techniques for reducing software risk.* Amsterdam: Elsevier

Dickinson B. (1989). *Developing Quality Systems: A Methodology Using Structured Techniques.* Maidenhead: McGraw Hill

DTI (1992). *Tick IT: Making a Better Job of Software -Guide to Software Quality Management SystemConstruction and Certification using EN 29001, Issue 2.0.* Department of Trade and Industry

Dunn R.H. (1990). *Software Quality: Concepts and plans.* Englewood Cliffs: Prentice Hall

Evans M.W. (1987). *Software Quality Assurance and Management.* Chichester: Wiley

Gillies A.C. (1992). *Software Quality - Theory and Management. London:* Chapman and Hall

Humphrey W. (1989). *Managing the Software Process.* Reading:

Addison-Wesley

Ince D. (1991). *Software Quality and Reliability: Tools and Methods.* London: Chapman and Hall

STRI TS2 (1991). *Modelling a Software Quality Handbook.* Icelandic Council for Standardization (STRá á, Iá ántá'áknistofnun á áslands, Keldnaholti, IS-112Reykjaváják, Iceland).

Watts R. (1987). *Measuring Software Quality.* Manchester: NCC Publication

Weinberg G. (1993). *Quality Software Management* vol. 1 & 2. Dorset House

Software Engineering References

Bell Canada (1992) *TRILLIUM* © *Telecom Software Product Development Capability Assessment Model.* Bell Canada

Boehm Barry. (1988). *A Spiral Model of Software Development and Enhancement.* IEEE May 1988

Brooks F.P. (1975). *The Mythical Man-Month.* Reading: Addison-Wesley

ESA (1991). *ESA Software Engineering Standards* Issue 2. ESA Publications Division, ESTEC, Noordwijk, The Netherlands.

ESA *ESS PSS-05 Software Engineering Series.* ESA Publications Division. ESTEC, Noordwijk, The Netherlands

Fenton N.E. (1991). *Software Metrics: A Rigorous Approach.* London: Chapman and Hall

Ghezzi C. (1991). *Fundamentals of Software Engineering.* Englewood Cliffs: Prentice Hall

Gilb T. (1988). *Principles of Software Engineering Management.* Wokingham: Addison-Wesley

Gilb T., Graham D. (1993). *Software Inspection.* Wokingham: Addison-Wesley

IEEE (1993). *IEEE Software Engineering Standards* 1993 Edition. The Institute of Electrical and Electronic Engineers

Macro A. (1990). *Software Engineering: Concepts and Management.* Englewood Cliffs: Prentice Hall

Paulk M. et al. (1993). *Capability Maturity Model for Software* Version 1.1. SEI, CMU/SEI-93-TR-24 and TR-25

Pressman R.S. *Software Engineering: A Practitioners' Approach.* Maidenhead: McGraw Hill

Ratcliff B. (1987). *Software Engineering Principles and Practices.* Oxford: Blackwell Scientific Publications

Thayer R.H. (1988). *Software Engineering Project Management.* IEEE Computer Society Press

Thayer R.H. (1990). *System and Software Requirements Engineering.* IEEE Computer Society Press

Appendix C
Definition of Quality
Characteristics

This appendix is taken from the draft international standard ISO/IEC 9126 Information Technology Software Product Evaluation Quality Characteristics and Guidelines for internal use. The lower level subcharacteristics are included there for information, and do not themselves form part of the standard.

C.1   Functionality

A set of attributes that bear on the existence of a set of functions and their specified properties. The functions are those that satisfy stated or implied needs.

Suitability
: Attribute of software that bears on the presence and appropriateness of a set of functions for specified tasks.
Note: Examples for appropriateness are task-oriented composition of functions from constituent sub-functions, capacities of tables.

Accuracy
: Attributes of software that bear on the provision of right or agreed results or effects.
Note: For example this includes the needed degree of precision of calculated values.

Interoperability
: Attributes of software that bear on its ability to interact with specified systems.
Note: Interoperability is used in place of compatibility in order to avoid possible ambiguity with replaceability.

Compliance	Attributes of software that make the software adhere to application-related standards or conventions or regulations in laws and similar prescriptions.
Security	Attributes of software that bear on its ability to prevent unauthorized access, whether accidental or deliberate, to programs and data.

C.2   Reliability

A set of attributes that bear on the capability of software to maintain its level of performance under stated conditions for a stated period of time.

Maturity	Attributes of software that bear on the frequency of failure by faults in the software.
Fault tolerance	Attributes of software that bear on its ability to maintain a specified level of performance in cases of software faults or of infringement of its specified interface. Note: The specified level of performance includes fail safe capability.
Recoverability	Attributes of software that bear on the capability to re-establish its level of performance and recover the data directly affected in case of a failure and on the time and effort needed for it.

C.3   Usability

A set of attributes that bear on the effort needed for use and on the individual assessment of such use by a stated or implied set of users.

Understandability	Attributes of software that bear on the users' effort for recognizing the logical concept and its applicability.
Learnability	Attributes of software that bear on the users' effort for learning its application (for example operation control, input, output).

Operability   Attributes of software that bear on the users'
                            effort for operation and operation control.

C.4   Efficiency

A set of attributes that bear on the relationship between the level of
performance of the software and the amount of resources used under
stated conditions.

Time behaviour   Attributes of software that bear on response
                            and processing times and on throughput rates
                            in performing its function.

Resource behaviour   Attributes of software that bear on the amount
                            of resources used and the duration of such use
                            in performing its function.

C.5   Maintainability

A set of attributes that bear on the effort needed to make specified
modifications.

Analyzability   Attributes of software that bear on the effort
                            needed for diagnosis of deficiencies or causes of
                            failures, or for identification of parts to be
                            modified.

Changeability   Attributes of software that bear on the effort
                            needed for modification, fault removal or for
                            environmental change.

Stability   Attributes of software that bear on the risk of
                            unexpected effect of modifications.

Testability   Attributes of software that bear on the effort
                            needed for validating the modified software.
                            Note: Values of this subcharacteristic may be
                            altered by the modifications under consider-
                            ation.

C.6 Portability

A set of attributes that bear on the ability of software to be transferred from one environment to another.

Adaptability   Attributes of software that bear on the opportunity for its adaptation to different specified environments without applying other actions or means than those provided for this purpose for the software considered.

Installability   Attributes of software that bear on the effort needed to install the software in a specified environment.

Conformance   Attributes of software that make the software adhere to standards or conventions relating to portability.

Replaceability   Attributes of software that bear on opportunity and effort of using it in place of specified other software in the environment of that software.
Note 1: Replaceability is used in place of compatibility in order to avoid possible ambiguity with interoperability.
Note 2: Replaceability with a specific software does not imply that this software is replaceable with the software under consideration.
Note 3: Replaceability may include attributes of both installability and adaptability. The concept has been introduced as a subcharacteristic of its own because of its importance.

Appendix D
Essential Practices Cross-referenced to ISO 9000–3

ISO 9000–3 Paragraph	Cross-reference to Key Practice (see Appendix E)
4. Quality System Framework	
4.1 Management Responsibility	MN(5) PM(1) QA(1-2) OL(16-17,24,27-30)
4.2 Quality System	OL(1)
4.3 Internal Quality System Audits	QA(3-4,7)
4.4 Corrective Action	VN(3) QA(6) OL(3-5,8,10-12,15)
5. Quality System Life Cycle Activities	
5.1 Contract Reviews	UR(4,7) SR(7) AD(10) PN(9,12)
5.2 Purchaser's Requirements Specification	UR(1-3,5-6,8)
5.3 Development Planning	SR(1) AD(7) PN(9,13) PM(2,7-9) VN(4)
5.4 Quality Planning	PM(2,4-5,8) VN(2,4)
5.5 Design and Implementation	SR(2-3,5) AD(1,17) PN(1,14) CM(12) VN(2)
5.6 Testing and Validation	PN(3-5) TR(1) CM(12) VN(4-5,7-11) QA(5)
5.7 Acceptance	TR(1) VN(6-7)
5.8 Maintenance	UR(1) SR(4) AD(12-16) PN(6-8) MN(1-4,6) CM(13)

ISO 9000-3 Paragraph	Cross-reference to Key Practice (see Appendix E)
6. Quality System Supporting Activities	
6.1 Configuration Management	UR(8) SR(6) AD(7) PN(2) MN(2) CM(1-4,13,15-16,20)
6.2 Document Control	CM(14) OL(14)
6.3 Quality Records PN(14-15) TR(2) MN(1) PM(9) VN(5) QA(10)	UR(4) SR(5,10) AD(17-18) CM(9,11)
6.4 Measurements	OL(7,9)
6.5 Rules, Practices and Conventions	PN(10) PM(6)
6.6 Tools and Techniques	PN(10) PM(6)
6.7 Purchasing	QA(8) OL(18-21)
6.8 Included Software Product	QA(8) OL(21)
6.9 Training	QA(11) OL(23,25)

Key:

UR	User Requirements	PM	Project Management	
SR	Software Requirements	CM	Configuration Management	
AD	Architectural Design	VN	Verification	
PN	Production	QA	Quality Assurance	
TR	Transfer	OL	Organization Level	
MN	Maintenance			

Appendix E
Summary of Essential Practices

User Requirements

UR1   User support and maintenance requirements are part of the user requirements definition.

UR2   The user retains full control over the definition of the user requirements.

UR3   The requirements definition is as complete and stable as possible.

UR4   All phase outputs are reviewed, and the results recorded.

UR5   A user requirements document is produced, giving a precise and consistent statement of all known user requirements.

UR6   The user requirements document gives a general description of what the user expects the software to do and defines all constraints that the user wishes to impose on any solution.

UR7   The review of the user requirements document involves appropriate representatives of the users, operators, developers and managers.

UR8   The user requirements document is maintained under adequate change control procedures.

Software Requirements

SR1   The activities of this phase are carried out in accordance with documented phase plans, with progress against the plans being tracked and documented at regular intervals.

SR2   The developer constructs a logical model of the

software system, which represents an abstract, implementation-independent solution.

SR3   The logical model is used as a basis for producing the software requirements.

SR4   The support service is as rigorously defined, designed and implemented as the software.

SR5   All phase outputs are reviewed, and the results recorded.

SR6   A Software Requirements document is produced and maintained under configuration management.

SR7   The Software Requirements document is complete and covers all user requirements stated in the User Requirements document.

SR8   The Software Requirements document avoids implementation details and terminology, except where there are user constraints to this effect.

SR9   The Software Requirements document describes system functions in terms of what they must do rather than how they must do it.

SR10   Progress reports, audit reports, configuration status accounts and other miscellaneous documents are archived.

Architectural Design

AD1   A physical model describing the design of the software in implementation terminology is developed.

AD2   Each design component has defined inputs, outputs and functions to perform.

AD3   Control and data flows between design components are documented with the design.

AD4   Data structures which interface components are documented and contain at least the following information:
- a description of each element of the data structure
- relationships between elements
- the range of possible values for each element
- initial values for each element

AD5   The support service specification and the support service delivery specifications are developed together.

AD6   The support service design is subject to the same quality principles as the software design.

AD7   The developed design is documented in an Architectural Design document, and maintained under change control procedures.

AD8   The Architectural Design document defines all of the major software components and the interfaces between them.

AD9   The Architectural Design document defines or references all external interfaces between the software and its operational environment.

AD10   The Architectural Design document is complete in as much as every Software Requirement can be traced to a design component.

AD11   The Architectural Design document is detailed enough to allow a detailed implementation plan covering the remainder of the development to be drawn up.

AD12   The design of the support service is documented in a Support Service Design document and describes the support service specification and delivery specification.

AD13   The service specification contains a complete and precise statement of the service which is to be provided and defines a standard of acceptability for each service characteristic.

AD14   The delivery specification defines the means and methods by which the service will be delivered.

AD15   The delivery specification identifies resource requirements for the service delivery and the extent to which the service delivery relies on third party services or products.

AD16   The delivery specification defines a standard of acceptability for each service delivery characteristic.

AD17   All phase outputs are reviewed, and the results documented.

AD18   Progress reports, audit reports, configuration status accounts and other miscellaneous documents are archived.

Production

PN1   A critical review is held upon the completion of the detailed design of a major software component to ensure it is ready for implementation.

PN2   The process of integrating the coded software components is controlled using defined configuration management procedures.

PN3 Detailed test designs, test cases and test procedures are developed for unit, integration, system and acceptance testing activities.

PN4 Integration tests are directed at verifying that all of the software's major components identified in the architectural design interface correctly.

PN5 System testing is directed at verifying that the software system complies with the objectives stated in the software requirements document.

PN6 Responsibility and authority for all support service activities are clearly defined.

PN7 Service staff have the technical knowledge and the communications skills to perform their duties effectively.

PN8 Material resources identified in the support service design have been acquired and are in place for the start of the service.

PN9 The detailed design is documented in a Detailed Design document.

PN10 The Detailed Design document defines or references design and coding standards and tools.

PN11 The Detailed Design document is complete and accounts for all software requirements stated in the software requirements document.

PN12 Software requirements which are not met or cannot be satisfied by the detailed design are traced back to their corresponding user requirements and are resolved with the user.

PN13 Phase outputs include all items necessary to execute and modify any part of the produced software.

PN14 All phase outputs are reviewed, and the results documented.

PN15 Progress reports, audit reports, configuration status accounts and other miscellaneous documents are archived.

Transfer

TR1 Acceptance tests are carried out in accordance with documented test plans, designs, cases and procedures.

TR2 Results of acceptance tests are recorded and documented.

Maintenance

MN1   All modifications and enhancements are carried out in accordance with defined maintenance standards and procedures which cover the logging, analysis, resolution, scheduling and tracking of problem occurrences and new requirements.

MN2   Software code and documentation continues to be subject to configuration management.

MN3   Software documentation and code remain consistent with each other throughout the operational life of the software.

MN4   Adequate support service levels are maintained.

MN5   All maintenance standards and procedures are regularly monitored and periodically reviewed for appropriateness and effectiveness.

MN6   The specification and the delivery of the support service are regularly reviewed to ensure that the support service continues to meet the users' needs.

Project Management

PM1   The team structure for the project is defined and documented.

PM2   The development phases are defined, together with entry/exit criteria and required inputs and outputs for each phase.

PM3   All assumptions, dependencies and constraints which have influenced the project objectives and priorities are recorded.

PM4   Risks that threaten the success of the project are identified, assessed and prioritized.

PM5   Plans to reduce risk levels are devised, monitored and re-evaluated as the project progresses.

PM6   The selection of project methods and tools, and the organization of configuration management and verification activities lie within the constraints of relevant organization-wide standards and procedures.

PM7   All project management activities are planned, documented and monitored.

PM8   Project management plans for each phase incorporate a Work Breakdown Structure which covers all software development activities for the phase, including verification activities.

PM9 Project progress is continually monitored and tracked against plans.

Configuration Management

CM1 All major software items, including designs, documentation, code and data, are subject to appropriate configuration management procedures.

CM2 Configuration management procedures establish a means of identifying, storing and changing software items throughout the life cycle.

CM3 Every configuration item has an identifier which distinguishes it from other items with different requirements or implementation.

CM4 The identifier of a configuration item includes a version number which identifies the stage of evolution of the item and which is updated as the item changes.

CM5 The configuration identification scheme is capable of accommodating new configuration items without requiring changes to the identifiers of existing items.

CM6 Each code module contains a header which, along with component information, contains a configuration item identifier, the original author and creation date of the module, and change history information consisting of a change date, author and description.

CM7 All documentation and storage media are labelled in a standard format which contains, at least, a project name, configuration identifier, date and content description.

CM8 To ensure adequate control and security of the software, at a minimum, development, master and static libraries are implemented for storing all deliverable software items.

CM9 Procedures for regular backup of development libraries are established.

CM10 Static libraries are never modified.

CM11 Up-to-date security copies of all master and static libraries are always available.

CM12 When a software item does not conform to specification, it is identified as non-conforming and is held for review action.

CM13 Appropriate procedures are in place to handle problem reports and change proposals, covering logging, analysis, approval of action, implementation and follow-up.

CM14 Procedures are in place for reviewing and approving documents (including procedures, plans and product-related documents) and changes to them, and for ensuring that relevant issues are available for use where and when required.

CM15 The status of all configuration items is recorded.

CM16 The date and status of each review report, change record, problem report and change request is recorded.

CM17 The first software release is documented in a software transfer document.

CM18 Subsequent software releases are accompanied by a software release note which records all faults that have been repaired and any new requirements that have been incorporated.

CM19 All modified software is retested before release.

CM20 For each release, documentation and code are consistent, and previous releases are archived.

Verification

VN1 Verification activities reflect the criticality of the software being developed.

VN2 Methods of detecting and removing defects, such as walkthroughs and inspections, are employed before testing.

VN3 Records of defects are analyzed to identify the causes of defects, and action is taken to eliminate them.

VN4 Plans are produced covering unit, integration, system and acceptance testing activities.

VN5 Detailed test designs, test cases, test procedures and test reports are produced covering unit, integration, system and acceptance testing.

VN6 Physical and functional audits of all external deliverables are performed before each software release.

VN7 Outline acceptance test plans are produced during the user requirements phase.

VN8 Outline system test plans are produced during the software requirements phase.

VN9 Outline integration test plans are produced during the architectural design phase.

VN10 Outline unit test plans are produced during the detailed design stage of the production phase.

VN11 All key software items are subject to verification to ensure that they conform to specification, and that all user requirements are engineered into the design and code of the software.

Quality Assurance

QA1 Quality assurance activities are performed by staff who are independent of the project.

QA2 The project management structure, and the defined roles and responsibilities within the structure, are validated.

QA3 Adherence to all project standards and practices is monitored throughout the project.

QA4 Project review and audit arrangements are examined to ensure that they are adequate and verify that they are appropriate.

QA5 Plans and reports relating to project testing activities are reviewed and validated.

QA6 Project error-handling procedures are reviewed and monitored to ensure that problems are tracked from identification right through to resolution, and elimination of the cause where possible.

QA7 The procedures, methods and facilities used to maintain, store, secure and document controlled versions of software are checked to be adequate and in use.

QA8 Externally acquired and contracted software is validated against project standards.

QA9 Each subcontractor is required to produce a quality assurance plan which can be checked and validated.

QA10 Adequate methods and facilities exist to assemble, safeguard and maintain all non-deliverable project related documentation.

QA11 All development staff are appropriately skilled for the tasks they are required to perform and any training needs are identified.

QA12 Software quality assurance plans are developed and documented.

Organization Level

OL1 A documented standard software process is established and maintained by the organization, which projects may tailor to their needs.

OL2   Staff and managers involved in using the software process are kept informed of process improvement activities.

OL3   A process for submitting, reviewing, approving and implementing process improvement proposals is established.

OL4   Changes to the documented standard software process are reviewed and approved by management.

OL5   Information about the outcome of completed projects is maintained in some form of software process library.

OL6   Information from completed projects is reviewed before being added to the software process library.

OL7   Measurements of the performance of the standard process, as applied by individual projects, are taken and analyzed.

OL8   Adjustments are made to the standard process, on the basis of performance analysis, with a view to stabilizing the performance of the process within acceptable limits.

OL9   Selected process and product metrics are linked to real customer requirements.

OL10 Defect prevention activities are included in each project's development plan and schedule.

OL11 At the level of the organization, trends which indicate broad problems across several projects are identified and documented and corrective action is taken to eliminate them.

OL12 Defect prevention activities are followed up and coordinated across the organization to ensure they have been implemented and are having the desired effect.

OL13 New technologies are monitored, evaluated and implemented as appropriate within the organization.

OL14 The organization's standard software process is maintained under configuration management and changes derived from various sources are documented, reviewed and approved by management.

OL15 Procedures for planning, approving, implementing, reviewing and tracking process improvement proposals are established and followed.

OL16 The status, adequacy and efficiency of the standard software process is periodically reviewed (at least annually).

OL17 The responsibilities for reviewing the standard

software process are clearly defined and assigned to designated managers and staff, and records of such reviews are maintained.

OL18 The organization develops and maintains procedures relating to the procurement of key inputs to the software process, and in particular to the purchasing and subcontracting of software.

OL19 The software standards, procedures and product requirements for subcontracted work comply with the prime contractor's commitments, and the prime contractor tracks the subcontractors' actual results and performance against them.

OL20 Suppliers are selected on the basis of their ability to meet stated requirements, and records of their performance are kept and used for selection when available.

OL21 Supplies are verified on receipt to ensure that they meet stated requirements. This includes items supplied by the customer.

OL22 The performance of subcontractors is periodically evaluated throughout the subcontract and the results of such reviews are recorded.

OL23 The organization develops training programmes to ensure that staff and managers have the skills and knowledge to perform their jobs and effectively use the capabilities and features of the work environment.

OL24 The training programmes are periodically reviewed and revised as necessary.

OL25 Each project develops and maintains a training plan which specifies its training needs and which identifies the set of skills needed or desired within the project.

OL26 Records detailing staff training histories and courses are maintained for use by management.

OL27 Management defines and documents its policy, objectives and commitment to quality and ensures that they are understood and implemented at all levels in the organization.

OL28 The responsibility, authority, and interrelation of all staff who manage, perform and verify work affecting quality is defined.

OL29 Management formally reviews the established quality system to ensure its continuing effectiveness and efficiency.

OL30 Management reviews of the quality system are documented.

Appendix F
Overview of the Capability Maturity Model

What is it?

The Capability Maturity Model is a framework that describes the elements of an effective software process and an evolutionary path that increases an organization's software process maturity. A fundamental principle underlying the CMM is that the quality of a software product can be improved by improving the process which produces it.

The framework therefore maps out a path which can be used by organizations to move from an ad hoc, chaotic process to a mature, disciplined process in several stages. Each stage provides the foundation on which to build improvements undertaken at the next stage. Therefore, the framework is a road-map for organizations embarking on the journey of continuous process improvement rather than a quick fix for projects in trouble.

Where Does it Come From?

The CMM is based on pioneering work on software process improvement carried out in the mid-eighties by Ron Radice and his colleagues working under the direction of Watts Humphrey at IBM. Humphrey took Philip Crosby's famous quality management maturity grid (which describes five evolutionary stages in adopting quality practices) and adapted it to the software process. In 1986, when he moved to the Software Engineering Institute (SEI), he brought this work with him and added the concept of maturity levels. In 1987, the SEI released a brief description of this process maturity framework along with a maturity questionnaire. Over the next four years, the framework was refined on the basis of industry feedback and the SEI's experience of using it, and was first published in 1991 as the Capability Maturity Model (see Appendix B).

How is it Structured?

Continuous process improvement is based on many small evolutionary steps rather than revolutionary innovations. The CMM provides a framework for organizing these steps into five maturity levels that lay successive foundations for continuous process improvement. A maturity level is a well-defined evolutionary plateau on the path toward becoming a mature software organization. Each level comprises a set of goals that, when satisfied, stabilize an important component of the software process.

There are five such maturity levels in the Capability Maturity Model. These are the Initial, Repeatable, Defined, Managed and Optimizing maturity levels.

Initial. The software process is characterized as ad hoc. Few processes are defined and success depends on individual effort.

Repeatable. Basic project management processes are established to track cost, schedule and functionality. The necessary process discipline is in place to repeat earlier successes on projects with similar applications.

Defined. The software process for both management and engineering activities is documented, standardized and integrated into an organization-wide software process. All projects use a documented and approved version of the organization's process for developing and maintaining software.

Managed. Detailed measures of the software process and product quality are collected. Both the software process and products are quantitatively understood and controlled using these measures.

Optimizing. Continuous process improvement is enabled by quantitative feedback from the process and from testing innovative ideas and technologies.

For each level, the model outlines a set of key process areas which must be satisfactorily addressed before an organization can be said to be at that level. In turn, each key process area is characterized by a set of key practices which address the implementation and

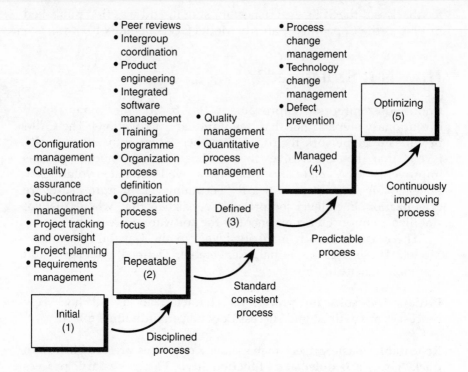

Figure F.1 Maturity levels and key process areas of the Capability Maturity Model.

institutionalization of the key process area.

An organization may tackle key process areas which are at higher levels than its maturity level, but, according to the SEI's argument, will not gain optimum benefit until it reaches that level. In addition, they argue that it is counterproductive to skip maturity levels because each level forms a necessary foundation from which to construct the next level. The reasoning goes something like this:

- A defined process cannot be successfully implemented before a repeatable process, since without the management discipline of a repeatable process, the engineering process will usually end up being sacrificed to schedule and cost pressures.
- A managed process cannot be successfully implemented before a defined process has been established, since without a defined process, there is no common basis for interpreting measurements.
- An optimizing process cannot be implemented before a managed process because without controlling the process within statistically narrow boundaries (small process measures) there is too much noise in the data to objectively determine whether a specific process improvement has an effect.

Index